5 STEPS TO
BOARD SUCCESS!

New Approaches To
Board Effectiveness and
Business Success

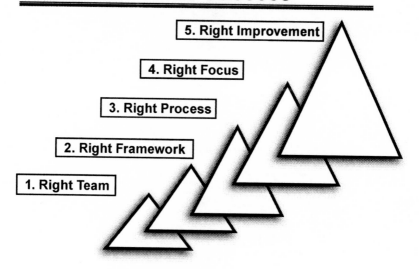

5. Right Improvement

4. Right Focus

3. Right Process

2. Right Framework

1. Right Team

By
Mark Daly

author**HOUSE**™

1663 LIBERTY DRIVE, SUITE 200
BLOOMINGTON, INDIANA 47403
(800) 839-8640
WWW.AUTHORHOUSE.COM

First published by AuthorHouse 04/20/05

ISBN: 1-4208-3822-9 (sc)
ISBN: 1-4208-3821-0 (dj)

Library of Congress Control Number: 2005902379

Printed in the United States of America
Bloomington, Indiana

This book is printed on acid-free paper.

Daly, Mark
        5 steps to board success! New approaches to board effectiveness and business success /
Mark Daly.
                p.   cm.
        Includes index and bibliography.
        ISBN 0-9717903-5-3
        1. Business. 2. Directors of corporations.
        3. Entrepreneurship. 4. Strategic planning.
        5. Family business.
        I. Title. II. Title: 5 steps to board success!
        III. Title: Five steps to board success! New approaches to board effectiveness and
        business success. IV. Title: Five steps to board success!

To
Gigi, my
wonderful wife.
I am truly blessed and
lucky to share life with you.
And to Gregg, Steven, and Patrick,
my incredible three sons. May each of you
have all of the successes in life you so deserve!

Love all ways and always

Acknowledgments

Heartfelt thanks goes out to my past business partners, Barb Ankenman, Brian Brumm, Tom Campbell, Mike Collette, Tod Herbers, Chris Hessler, Rick Granato, Breck Jones, Mike McAllister, Dr. Kevin O'Brien, Deborah Schnell, Walter Solomon, Gary Steier, and Charlie Vogel. Each of you has provided a real-world learning lab and helped me as I stumbled along the learning curve. In particular, Brian Brumm generously reviewed several drafts of this book and provided many useful suggestions.

A further debt is owed to Bill Connell, Bob Donovan, Nate Levinson, Bruce Moody, and Norm Sherman, board members who have provided great advice, support, and insight, and to John Steele, Thom Gerdes, Lisa FitzGibbon, Lee Reading, Sid Barton, and Ed VonderBrink, who asked me to serve on their boards. Bill Connell graciously reviewed drafts of the book and provided very helpful suggestions.

Young Presidents' Organization (YPO) has served as a fountain of inspiration over the years. Members Bob Scallan, Jim Akers, and Wym Portman epitomize the YPO vision of "better leaders though education and idea exchange." Bob, Jim, and Wym provided excellent suggestions and offered encouragement.

Many people generously invested precious time to read drafts of the manuscript, make helpful suggestions, provide support and encouragement, and/or share excellent ideas that helped to shape and improve this work, including Jim Akers, Ed Alf, Lesley Bolton, Brian Brumm, JB Buse, Jim Bushman, Phil Castellini, Jim Collins, Steve Cobb, Bill Connell, Scott Cook, Gigi Daly, Gregg Daly, David Deye, Bob Dieckman, Dave Dillon, David Drees, Dave Dupee, Lisa FitzGibbon, Neil Ganulin, Thom Gerdes, Jim Graves, Doug Hall, Jeb Head, Tod Herbers, Sherrie Human, Ph.D., David Lewis, Brian McHale, Rene McPherson, Les Overway, Terri Phillips, Wym Portman, Art Powell Sr., Stephen Ramirez, Mike Rorie, Bob Scallan,

Tom Shepherd, Norm Sherman, John Smale, Walter Solomon, Joanne Spigner, John Steele Jr., Steve Steinman, Chris Taylor, Ed VonderBrink, John L. Ward, John Winch, Jay Woodhull II and many others through the research phase of the book. Thanks, you are the best!

There are several very special people I'd also like to acknowledge. First is Les Overway, who has formally guided me (as my first boss at P&G) and informally guided me as my friend and mentor through lunchtime learning sessions.

Second is Jim Collins, a student of enduring great companies who has created several business book masterpieces. He gave me the following challenge (paraphrased), "imagine if you knew you were going to die but could work on your book until you got it to a level that you wanted before you died—imagine the book being your gift to the world, what else would you do now to make it great?" Jim, thank you for the challenge. It led to significant refinement that would not have occurred without your thoughtful prod.

Third is John Ward. John is one of the leading authorities on family businesses. Having had the pleasure of serving on a board with him, I can say firsthand that John is also one of the best board members you will find anywhere. I learned a ton from him. John has also been very supportive with this book. John, thanks for the guidance and your selfless help.

Last and most is Gigi, my wife, who has an uncanny ability to correctly read people, and who has provided invaluable advice, support, and patience, without which this publication and my life would not be complete.

Contents

(Step 4) THE RIGHT BOARD FOCUS

(Step 5) THE RIGHT BOARD IMPROVEMENT

SPECIAL BOARD CONSIDERATIONS

CONCLUSIONS

APPENDIX AND RESOURCES

1. Introduction

"Give a man a fish and you feed him for a day. Teach a man to fish and he can feed himself for a lifetime."

— Chinese Proverb

1. Introduction

A Roadmap for Success

With constant change and competition, it is difficult to *consistently* make the best business decisions. A board can help your business win more and lose less... if done right. Perhaps you considered creating an advisory board but were not sure how to best go about it... or you already have a board of directors, but the business is not earning as much money as you would like.

Whether you are involved with an entrepreneurial, family, or professionally managed small to midsize private business, continue reading to discover new, effective tools and techniques for board and business success.

As in life, there are no guarantees. However, this book concisely explains how you can start or run a peak-performing board using the five "right" steps. As a result, you can outsmart your competition, earn more profit, and gain more control over your business's destiny. An effective board should also reduce stress and loneliness associated with running a business.

Surprisingly, many businesses have not yet discovered the many benefits that can accrue by leveraging a highly effective board. Those that do it right reap big rewards. Concrete evidence of this emerged through personal experience, quantitative survey research, and extensive interviews conducted by the author among business leaders, business experts, and board members.

According to Jay Woodhull II (former President of IKON Office Solutions), *"I wish I had implemented a board at my first company. I would have gotten there faster and not felt the intense loneliness as a president. An outside board would have made the experience much more rewarding and enriching."*

A lot of learning has emerged from the survey research and interviews conducted among business leaders. Their approaches to boards can be sorted into one of three camps—those that:

1. *Had highly effective boards;*
2. *Had less effective boards;*
3. *Did not have boards.*

Camp # 1: Highly Effective Boards; "The Wise Few"

Only 10 percent of business leaders surveyed fell into this camp. However, this select group *raved* about their boards. First of all, profitability was higher than competitors and benchmarks. Beyond the bottom line, testimonials flowed how their boards provided confidence and support. The leaders were *inspired* to aim high. They praised their boards for reflecting truth and providing a heavy dose of candor.

They boasted how their boards helped them discover game-changing strategies and brought fresh ideas to outsmart competition. As a result, these business leaders are more successful and profitable today.

All told, twelve persuasive benefits of a board were voiced among the business leaders, business experts, and board members who were interviewed. Their good practices are echoed throughout this book, along with many other ideas and suggestions. The twelve benefits are presented in Chapter 2 *(Discover the Twelve Benefits of a Good Board)*.

Importantly, even if you believe you have an effective board, this book can help you become more successful. Those who had highly effective boards shared ideas and suggestions. Why not leverage their wisdom contained herein?

Camp # 2: Less Effective Boards; "Unknowing Errors"

Most business leaders surveyed fell into the "less effective boards" camp. Through the interviews and research, it was found that many "errors" were committed without the knowledge of the participants.

The good news is that these "unknowing errors" can be prevented. They can also be corrected. Perhaps the biggest was the lack of attention paid to finding the *right* board members. A number of business leaders had "recruited friends." Boards were cluttered with "insiders" who lacked specific expertise to help the business grow to the next levels of success. In fact, only 30 percent of those surveyed had a majority of independent directors.*

Another error was a lack of sharing appropriate information with the board. This tended to reduce trust and prevent healthy dissension during board meetings and discussions.

When asked about the board's purpose, a number of business leaders gave vague answers. Holding management accountable to results was seldom voiced as a reason to have an outside (independent) board.

What's more, only 22 percent of those surveyed had drafted a clear set of expectations for their boards (based on the Board Governance Survey noted above).

Many business leaders and board members did not manage board meeting time well. Meeting preparation was often lacking. Just as problematic, at times, the meeting process was not disciplined. When asked what was discussed in typical board meetings, it became apparent that precious time evaporated while reporting or rehashing less significant information. When asked why higher-level strategic

* Data is based on a Board Governance Survey that was conducted by the author in August, 2004 among a broad range of small to midsize U.S. businesses that had at least fifty employees and sales that ranged from $5 million on the low side to over $1 billion on the high side. $n = 112$

and policy issues were not tackled, a common response was "We ran out of time."

Lastly, through the research, it was found that *only 12 percent* of the boards went through a formal evaluation process. Consequently, it was difficult for them, if not impossible, to have effective board improvement plans in place.

Net, the "errors" noted above are correctable. This book provides you with step-by-step tools so that you avoid these mistakes and others. Learn how to find, attract, and retain the *best* board team for your unique business needs. See the importance of establishing a highly trusted board of experts, one that infuses independent strategic expertise into your business so that it thrives. Uncover new tools to run focused, productive board meetings and to develop a useful board constitution. The *15 Key Strategic Questions* every business should ask to keep board discussions focused on the highest return strategies will be revealed. Plus, you will find tips on how to properly manage, compensate, evaluate, and improve the board so that it is genuinely motivated to continually grow your business.

Camp # 3: No Boards; "Fear or an Unclear Path"

Too many business leaders fell into the "no boards" camp. For perspective, nearly 29 percent of the companies surveyed did not have a board (either an advisory or a formal statutory board). Even more surprising was the fact that a number of these companies had annual sales volume in excess of $50 million. These leaders identified a host of concerns as to why they did not have a board, concerns which boiled down to either fear or not knowing how to best go about creating a board.

Their specific concerns form the basis of Chapter 3 *(Overcome Your Concerns with Creating a Board)*. After discussing their concerns, many believed they were unfounded. Virtually all of the business leaders agreed that the effort to establish a board would be well worth the return. They just wanted a roadmap to help them succeed and knowledge to overcome their concerns.

Boards Help Businesses Win

Technically, a board's purpose is to protect and represent the interests of the shareholders (owners). That is an important purpose. However, there is another valuable purpose—*to infuse independent expertise and strategic advice that helps the business win long-term* (in other words, grow and earn more profit than the competition, over time).

The essential "game" of business is to continually invent (e.g. achieve product, operations, marketing, distribution, customer, financial, technological, and other improvements) so that the business *maximizes profit over time*. Continuous and increasing profit is concrete evidence of lasting value creation—of winning. It is a good scorecard of business success.

There are nearly 500,000 U.S.-based businesses with between 25 and 999 employees.* The main purpose of this book is to help these and other American businesses discover winning strategies and achieve breakthrough results through their boards. With the right tools and techniques, and proper board input, these businesses can become more profitable (successful) over time. As a result, America will become more competitive.

Family and Entrepreneurial Businesses Have Special Board Needs

An important observation realized through numerous discussions with family and entrepreneurial business leaders and through personal board experience is that family and entrepreneurial businesses have special needs. Family business leaders revealed complicated, dysfunctional situations where family members and the business had misaligned agendas. Entrepreneurs were running into challenging transitions due to hyper-growth. Thus, both can truly benefit from an outside board. To address these and other special needs, specific chapters are dedicated to family businesses

* Source: U.S. Small Business Administration, Office of Advocacy, based on U.S. Census Bureau, Statistics of U.S. Businesses.

and entrepreneurs (Chapters 20, *Family Business Matters* and 21, *The Entrepreneur's Board*).

Board Members Want and Need Help

Board members who were interviewed expressed keen interest in practical suggestions that would help them perform better. While this book is written to the heads and hearts of small to midsize business leaders, it should provide a useful framework on how to excel in the role of a small to midsize business board member.

There are helpful resources sprinkled throughout the book and in the Appendix, such as specific role descriptions, performance evaluations, checklists, and tips. These tools will guide board members so that they are more successful in their board roles. Chapter 6 defines what makes great board members, and Chapter 22 *(Tips for Serving on Other Boards)* will assist potential board members in thinking through the decision to join a board or not, and if they decide to join, how they can hit the ground running.

Principles Apply to Large Companies Too

The advice contained within this book is targeted towards private businesses that are midsize and smaller. However, many of the board effectiveness principles described herein also apply to larger, publicly traded businesses. Regardless of size, most businesses face similar issues—growth, competition, adequate financial resources, technological opportunities, finding and keeping good people, improving marketing, sales and operational effectiveness, growing profits, and the like. The problems are similar; the differences are a matter of complexity and scale.

A Definition

Before we proceed, let's define a business board as follows: *"A high-performance select team of mostly independent experts whose collective responsibilities are to infuse strategy and policy advice that helps the business win more over time and maximize long-term shareholder value."*

Related to the above definition, a board should have three or more independent "experts." More than half of the total members should be independent. The power of an independent board is realized by leveraging the right team of independent experts to move the business ahead. There should be a conscious effort to create a high-performance team with specific and diverse independent expertise. That expertise should be tailored to the unique needs of growing the business.

A Few Communication Caveats

For simplicity in communication, throughout this book, the term "board" will be used to refer to an *independent* board of directors for a small to midsize company, unless specified otherwise. Additionally, "board" will be used interchangeably to refer to an advisory board and a statutory board of directors with the understanding that there are *definite* legal and other very material differences between these two forms of boards (which are detailed in Chapter 9, *Establish the Right Board for Your Business Needs*).

A Pragmatic Approach

The approach to this book is straightforward. It breaks the path to board success into five steps. Each step is designed to make it easier for you to lead a successful board:

Step 5: Right Improvement Purposefully monitor then develop effective board improvement plans.

Step 4: Right Focus Focus board discussions on strategy and policy issues (doing the right things).

Step 3: Right Process Prepare for and organize meetings with discipline and rigor (doing things right). Build trust through open communication.

Step 2: Right Framework Set up the right independent board for your business needs. Establish clear expectations, fair compensation and insurance.

Step 1: Right Team Recruit a team of experts who are most qualified to help your business achieve its long-term vision, objectives, and goals.

My wish is that this book inspires you to passionately take action to reach the top of your business success with the help of a peak-performing board.

Mark Daly
Mark@DalySA.com
Cincinnati, Ohio
March 15, 2005

DECIDING TO FORM A BOARD

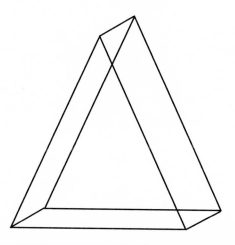

This section covers the key considerations in deciding to form a board. It begins with a chapter on the twelve persuasive benefits of boards. The next chapter covers common concerns with forming a board. The final chapter in this section provides an overview of the 5 Steps that will lead you to a peak-performing board.

2. Discover the Twelve Benefits of a Good Board

"Smart people learn from experience, wise people learn from the experience of others"

— Dr. Ichak Adizes, author and innovator in organizational transformations

2. Discover the Twelve Benefits of a Good Board

Are You Open to the Possibilities?

Too many American businesses are not leveraging the power of an independent board. According to the Board Governance Survey conducted by the author, over 29 percent of small to midsize companies do not have an advisory or statutory board. Even more surprising, a number of the companies without boards had annual sales in excess of $50 million. This is unfortunate.

When asked why they did not have a board, the business leaders identified a variety of concerns. These concerns can be summarized as either "fear," or not knowing how to best go about creating a board. The business leaders did not realize that they could be more successful with an effective, independent board.

To help overcome the concerns, this chapter reveals the twelve benefits of a "good" board. Each of the twelve is compelling. When you add them together, the argument for a board becomes very persuasive.

The word "good" was chosen in an effort to not oversell the benefits. Judgmentally, that's because even an average (good) board can help your business be more successful. However, let us not be satisfied with good. There is no reason why you cannot have a peak-performing board if you follow the advice in this book and add your own real-world experiences and wisdom to it. The following are the twelve benefits of a good board.

1. Expert, Objective Advice

A good board brings much-needed competencies and expert advice to your business. The proficiencies of each board member broaden perspectives and facilitate making better decisions. Good board members provide multiple sets of "fresh eyes," all focused on supporting you to achieve greatness while advising you to confront reality. Those fresh eyes bring an independent, unbiased lens to your business.

2. Vital, Strategic Advice

A good board encourages you to focus on important long-term issues, ensuring you have the right team, core values, purpose, mission, strategies, policies, growth initiatives, competitive advantages, and the like. It is critical for any business to be headed in the right direction. Following the right strategy is a must for long-term success. A good board helps you to begin with the end in mind so that your plans are tied to long-term outcomes and the company's purpose and mission. A good board also helps ensure that your plans for the future remain alive. Complacency is a death-knell for any businesses. A good board prevents a business from becoming complacent.

3. Helps Invent

In the long term, companies that invent rather than imitate are more likely to be true winners. A good board helps you invent. It provides out-of-the-box ideas and solutions. It identifies unique opportunities, approaches, and perspectives. Likewise, it serves as an objective sounding board to explore new ideas.

A good board asks the right questions to determine if the leaders have the right boundaries for the business. It also challenges and pushes the boundaries of the leaders' thinking.

4. Reduces Risk

A good board helps you identify the major risks to the business. It is very beneficial to have *wise* people (experts) on your team who can help you see hazards so that you can safely navigate through them. Even more important, this wisdom can prevent you from getting into high-risk situations in the first place.

5. Protects Shareholder Interests

A good board looks after the interests of all shareholders. It seeks to maximize long-term shareholder value. In fact, protecting shareholder interests is a legal responsibility of statutory boards. This duty is mandated by corporate law in every state and most countries. Of note, protecting shareholder interests does not *legally* apply to advisory boards. This and other very real differences between these two forms of boards will be discussed in Chapter 9 *(Establish the Right Board for Your Business Needs)*.

6. Defines the Priorities

Every business gets caught up in mundane activity. Unfortunately, this useless activity can trick us into believing we are accomplishing something worthwhile. However, if activity is not focused on the right outcomes and strategies, we can easily spin our wheels and lose traction.

A good board helps you deal with the important versus the seemingly urgent. It assists you in putting first things first. It is easy to fall into the trap of fighting in-your-face, day-to-day tactics. Independent experts who are not as close to your business can help you define *the right priorities* so that the business does not waste time, and maximizes its potential.

7. Expands Networks

You can easily pay for your board with the networking advantages it can provide. A good board should significantly increase the scope and value of your contact list. Specifically, it can expand your network in the following areas:

❖ Strategic partnership, acquisition, or divestiture leads
❖ Competitive intelligence leads
❖ Sales and new customer leads/contacts
❖ Market research and information leads
❖ International connections

7

- ❖ Knowledge sources (articles, books, Web sites, people, organizations, associations, and the like)
- ❖ Sources of employee talent
- ❖ Financing and capital leads
- ❖ Benchmarking leads
- ❖ Consultant and other external resource leads
- ❖ New supplier leads
- ❖ Outsourcing leads
- ❖ Introductions to government officials
- ❖ Sources for additional board member candidates
- ❖ Succession and exit opportunities

8. Fosters Accountability

A major accountability issue encountered in small to midsize businesses is that there rarely is an objective third party evaluating performance. Business leaders can operate in a self-preserved kingdom without being held accountable for their actions. Mediocrity sets in. Profitability suffers. Shareholder value suffers. Everyone loses.

A good board can hold the CEO and executive team *accountable* to the right results—in bad and good times. This accountability invariably leads to higher performance and greater success (winning).

9. Enhances Credibility

A good board can bring a valuable currency to your business; credibility. This is particularly true with start-up and smaller businesses. If you have some heavy hitters on your board, you can cut through the clutter. You can get noticed by investors, customers, suppliers, bankers, and potential employees. Like the networking benefit noted above, enhanced credibility can provide an excellent return on your investment in an independent board.

A good board also improves credibility and legitimacy among existing employees. The involvement of an independent board adds considerably to employees' pride, confidence, and hope for the future of the company. It sends a message that company leadership wants to be the best it can be. It helps instill respect for the CEO and the executive team.

10. Excellent Return on Investment (ROI)

A good board is an *efficient* way to glean *ongoing* expert advice. Once the board is oriented to your business, strategy, and policy issues, then it is easy to bring the board up to speed as your game plan unfolds. Net, a good board can provide an excellent return on your investment. Tenfold returns are common. Hundredfold returns are not uncommon.

11. Reduces Loneliness

With an advisory board or a board of directors, your business journey will not be as lonely. You will have someone to call for help and assistance. A team of experts will be there for you during the down times. They will also be there to help you celebrate the successes.

12. Improves Results

Perhaps most important, as an outcome of benefits 1 through 11, a good board will positively affect the right results such as profits, cash flow, market share, and shareholder value.

Profits and positive cash flow are the lifeblood of any business. Strong profitability is concrete evidence of value creation. It is an essential score of business success. There are many excuses, but few acceptable reasons for not achieving profitability over time. The start-up or investment phase of a new product, service, or business is a legitimate reason to initially sacrifice profit, but only for a limited period of time. If a business goes for a prolonged period of time without earning profit, then there is a fundamental problem with the business model and/or the executive team. A good board will help the business deliver the right results.

3. Overcome Your Concerns with Creating a Board

"If you are able to state a problem, then the problem can be solved."

—Edwin H. Land, American inventor, photographic pioneer and founder of the Polaroid Corporation

3. Overcome Your Concerns with Creating a Board

There are many perceived obstacles, barriers, or concerns that prevent business leaders from establishing effective advisory or statutory boards. Below is a list of common concerns that were voiced during the research phase of this book. They are paraphrased mostly from business leaders who resisted forming an outside board. Even if you have an existing board, you may want to review their concerns. After each concern, you will find considerations that may help to address the specific concern.

If you do not currently have a board, putting one together will likely require a change in your business practices. Sometimes, change can be difficult to accept.

There is an intriguing and easy-to-understand book by Ken Blanchard and Spencer Johnson, listed in the Appendix, called *Who Moved My Cheese?* It was a bestseller for good reason. The authors tell a parable of two mice. One mouse waited for the cheese to come; another chose to venture out and get the cheese. The moral of the story: the authors suggest we *choose* to take action and control our future versus waiting and reacting to bad things that will eventually *happen* to us.

Choosing to change the way you obtain expert advice and ideas could be one of the better decisions you make for your business. There are countless testimonials from executives (including the author) on the successes derived from boards. Many say that their main regret with their boards is that they did not create them sooner. If they had embraced change earlier, they would have enjoyed better results today.

"I Don't Want to Lose Control"

Given a glance, an independent board could appear restrictive and controlling. However, if done right, a good board will actually increase control over your destiny.

No one would dispute the fact that we feel trapped when the business is in a crisis mode or spiraling out of control. A good board will help prevent you from getting into these dire situations in the first place. Board members are on *your* team. They want you to compete in the right game and to win. As a result, you should realize more business success and financial freedom over time.

If you are concerned with handling uncontrolled criticism, ask yourself this question: *Which criticism do you prefer handling, listening to a group of experts who are on your team who provide objective, useful advice before or when problems occur, or listening to criticism from shareholders, customers, or employees because you made the wrong strategy or policy choices for your business?* The latter scenario can have far graver consequences than hearing criticism from your board. Specifically, there may be financial, legal, personal, and moral consequences to face.

Yes, a good board can provide candid and direct feedback, but isn't it better to know the unvarnished truth than to be misguided by a false sense of reality? A good board is like a personal mirror. It does not lie. It is there to reveal the hard realities to you within the confines and safety of your boardroom.

Thus, contrary to the illusion that a business leader will lose control or be "exposed," a board gives the leader the "ammo" to better control his or her destiny. When the business leader uses board meetings to effectively pick the board's brains, the leader retains the power to act on any, all, or none of the board's advice.

"I Don't Want to Put My Job in Jeopardy"

A related concern to losing control is the fear of putting your job in jeopardy. This is an understandable but potentially unfounded worry for a closely held (private) business. First of all, in private companies, it is uncommon to find examples where boards removed the business leaders. Another point to consider is that in many smaller businesses, the business leaders are typically substantial shareholders. With a statutory board, shareholders have the authority to elect the board, which in turn, elects the officers of the company.

However, the best defense against potentially losing your job is demonstrated strong performance. Remember, a board is there to help the business and you succeed. It is in the business leader's control to listen to and act upon the board's good advice. According to Dave Dillon (CEO of Kroger, who has served on both large public company and smaller private business boards) *"the real insurance is performance ... I would rather have my future in a good board's hands."*

Lastly, if you lead a private business and you are still concerned, there may be options to minimize the potential that your job can be taken away by a board through the creation of a close corporation agreement or a limited liability corporation (LLC). Check with your attorneys regarding specific approaches to restructure the organization to minimize board control. However, recognize that if you pursue these approaches, you may be forfeiting one of the most important of the twelve benefits of a good board namely, *accountability*.

If you are creating an advisory board, then you have little fear of losing your job as a result of the advisory board. An advisory board has no legal authority to dismiss the business leaders. In fact, unlike a statutory or legal board, technically, an advisory board has virtually no legal powers. Thus, it has very limited liability, a real plus when trying to recruit great experts to a private business board. It also can provide many of the twelve benefits of a good board if the *5 Steps* are properly followed.

"Boards Are Not Effective"

It's unfair to make a generalized statement such as "boards are not effective" based on limited experience, partial information covered by biased news media reports or a few bad apples. Some boards are very effective. Others are not. Any board can be effective but it is only as effective as:

- ❖ The quality of the board's members, including the leader; typically the CEO in a closely held business. (Step 1: *Right Team*)
- ❖ The board's framework or organizational structure, expectations, and parameters under which a board operates. (Step 2: *Right Framework*)
- ❖ The board's processes—the disciplined flow of activity with respect to efficiently and effectively managing the board towards desired results. (Step 3: *Right Process*)
- ❖ The board's focus—if the board works on the highest leverage activities or not. (Step 4: *Right Focus*)
- ❖ The board's improvement—how well the board analyzes its performance and purposefully improves itself. (Step 5: *Right Improvement)*

You may perceive that boards are not effective due to a bad experience serving on a board. Just because you have had a bad experience on another board, that does not mean your board has to perform poorly. One thing you have going for you is the tangible experience of what not to do. This book should add to your experiences. It should help you avoid committing "unknowing errors" or making mistakes.

Here's another point to consider. States require a private corporation to establish a statutory board to act as the official voice on the company's financial, legal, and management matters. If your business is incorporated, why not leverage your board to work to its maximum advantage?

"I'm Not Sure I Can Attract Good Candidates"

Getting good board candidates takes effort. However, if you approach the important step of pursuing the right experts (Step 1, *Right Team*), with advice found in this book, your task will be easier.

The first thing to do is to have an open mind and a positive attitude. If you are open to the possibility that an independent board can help you become a better business leader, outsmart competition, earn more money over time, and achieve more control over your business's destiny, you are well on your way to finding and attracting good board candidates.

It may seem like a daunting task. You may ask, "Why would anyone want to spend time on my business?" You would be surprised. Great board members tend to have a *passion* for business. They participate on boards because they like to help. They have a thirst to learn and contribute. If you clearly define what you are looking for and read Chapter 8 on how to recruit and retain great members, you will be well equipped. With a little focused effort, the right board experts are out there. They are approachable. Another point to consider when starting a new board is that you do not have to fill all the positions at once. Lastly, if there are unusual liability concerns, you may want to consider an advisory board. You will likely attract better candidates without the fiduciary and other burdens of a statutory board.

"I'm Too Busy ... Just Don't Have Time"

An effective board can actually save you time. Clearly, most business leaders have a very full plate. There are many priorities. It never seems like there is enough time to tackle everything on the "to do" list. Creating an effective board does require an investment in time. However, it should actually save you time over the long haul. If your business pursues the wrong path, you will end up wasting considerable time and energy trying to manage through crises. A board can help you identify more options and solutions to your business opportunities and challenges. Even more important, it can prevent crises from occurring in the first place, and keep you out of trouble.

"An Outside Board Seems Costly"

A private business board is not free. However, the returns on a nominal investment are typically outstanding. My board has more than paid for itself through significant savings in executive recruiter fees alone. For example, the lead for an experienced chief operating officer (COO) for ProtoCall (a business I co-founded) was suggested by a board member. Not only did the board member provide the lead, he also helped with introductions and provided credibility that the job was a good fit so that the COO would consider a move to a smaller startup company. It is unlikely that a great executive recruiter could have done as well in that situation. Net, ProtoCall was able to identify and recruit a better-qualified candidate—one who was essential to the success of the company, and there were no executive recruiter fees involved.

Here's another personal example of the potential high ROI that an independent board can garner. During the early stages of ProtoCall, a board member provided a high level introduction to a key client prospect. The board member's credibility provided a powerful networking benefit. That introduction cost the business nothing. It helped put ProtoCall in business through the signing of its first meaningful contract (over $300,000). That initial contract evolved into a greater than $3 million annual contract that renewed for many years. Net, the return on the investment in the ProtoCall board exceeded a hundredfold.

On a related point, how do you calculate the value of board advice that prevents you from entering a flawed market? During the dotcom euphoria, another company the author was involved in (On Target Media, Inc.) was considering Internet options for its healthcare media business. The board asked the right question: "Is there a supportable long-term Internet business model in your industry?" At that time, *drkoop.com* was trading at stratospheric stock price multiples. The board focused management to look at the long-term business model, not short-term stock prices. Time has proven the wisdom of that question. It demonstrated one of the "hidden" values of an outside board.

And how do you calculate the hidden returns of not entering a flawed market? A personal regret is not setting up a board when my first business was started. It likely would have advised an earlier exit. This mistake was very costly to me financially and in terms of lost opportunities.

Arguably, it is too costly to not invest in an independent board. A typical investment in a small to midsize private business board is approximately $75,000 per year (excluding long-term incentives and insurance). The investment is minimal compared to the potential returns. Net, tenfold and higher returns are feasible and commonly achieved.

"Board Members Don't Want the Liability"

This is a legitimate concern that needs to be dealt with. However, there are ways to minimize board member liabilities. An advisory board is an option that virtually eliminates this concern. What's more, if a business has good ethical practices and honest people, potential board member liability issues are less likely. Nonetheless, we do live in a litigious society. To that end, directors and officers (D&O) insurance is a potential solution to help protect the board and the business from liability fears. This will be covered in more detail in Chapter 12 *(Protect Your Board Members)*.

"Our Business Is Too Small to Consider an Outside Board"

Every great business started with a nucleus—a founder or a few employees. If your aspirations are to grow, your company can immediately benefit from an outside board. If you anticipate growing to twenty-five or more employees or you have a high revenue-per-employee business model, you should consider an outside board sooner rather than later.

You do not have to start with an elaborate or large board. In fact, Chapter 21 *(The Entrepreneur's Board)* suggests initially starting with only two to three independent advisors. You can easily add members as business needs evolve. It is prudent to establish a board early on, when a company is in its infancy, *before* it goes through major transitions or makes poor strategic or policy choices.

"Outsiders Won't Know My Business"

This statement is partially correct. Perhaps it is one of the best reasons to have a board of independent experts. One of the hallmarks of a good board is that it focuses on the "big picture," longer-term issues, not the intimate details of your business. It sees opportunities, in part because it is not encumbered by the day-to-day paradigms of the business. It can discern the forest from the trees.

Having an independent board that does not know your business as well as you can be an advantage—the members typically look at your business with "fresh eyes." Optimally, a board has a variety of experts on it. This "team of experts" brings more ideas, options and solutions to your business challenges or opportunities.

"Already Have a Board, Albeit It's Filled with Insiders"

If you have an "inside" board (one filled with mostly inside members), odds are, it is not as effective as it can be. It may actually be acting as a management team in disguise. If you create a truly handpicked independent board of experts, you will likely obtain more objective strategic guidance than from a board made up of insiders. Chapter 7 *(Keys to Identifying Great Board Members)* will provide clear parameters as to what to look for in identifying the right independent board experts.

Another point to consider is the ratio of insiders to outsiders (independent members). Cluttering a board with insider members defeats a prime purpose of a good board; namely *infusing independent expertise and strategic advice into your business.*

What should you do if you already have an inside board that is not very effective? There is no excuse for maintaining a poor-performing board. If you have a poor-performing board, make the right choice. Change your board. You and the business will be rewarded with more success.

Chapter 18 *(How to Evaluate Board Effectiveness)* contains a useful diagnostic tool that will help you identify the areas where your board is strong. It will also show areas where it can be improved. This analysis is a good starting place to improve or replace a poor-performing board.

"My Management Team Won't Like It"

An independent board is different than an internal executive (or management) team. An independent board is primarily focused on high-leverage, long-term issues such as strategy and policy. It also plays a monitoring, reviewing, and ratifying role. It does not play a day-to-day management role. The executive team typically takes care of the day-to-day tactics of a business. The roles of an independent board and an executive team complement and support each other.

Therefore, management should not feel threatened. An independent board is not there to second-guess day-to-day decisions. The board chairperson needs to keep this in check. The board is a resource to help ensure the company plays in the right game and has the right game plan. If management truly objects to an independent board, you should be concerned. Why are they threatened? Are there skeletons in the closet that they fear will be uncovered?

An impartial board should be seen as a benefit to management. It should also demonstrate that the leaders are open to the best advice for the company that can be obtained. An independent board should have no interest in gaining power. It is there to help the business achieve its objectives. An independent board is a trusted ally. Its interests are aligned with management.

"Family Members (or Shareholders) May Object"

There are three main reasons family members or shareholders may object to an independent board. One common objection is that family members feel their position may be worse off (i.e. they do not believe a board can help the business). The second common objection is that

21

they do not trust the board members. A lesser concern sometimes encountered is that they may perceive family matters to be private matters. However, good independent boards should be able to keep legitimate non-business-related family matters out of the boardroom.

To overcome the first objection, it may be worth reviewing the benefits covered in Chapter 3 *(Overcome Your Concerns with Creating a Board)* with family members or shareholders who have expressed concerns. Another approach is to share this book with them. If they understand that an independent board is there to look after their interests, then this objection should go away. However, it is important to recognize that it may take time to fully convince family members or shareholders who have expressed concerns with an outside board. Therefore, give them time to appreciate the value of a good board of independent experts.

As to trust concerns, it is important that the family members or shareholders understand who is on the board. A Board Search Description can help define who you are looking for (see Appendix 1 for an example). Showing them that you are not padding the board with a bunch of management-pleasing friends will go a long way to instilling trust. Having family members or shareholders periodically meet the board can also alleviate fears.

"I Don't Want to Share Private Information With Outsiders"

There are a few legitimate reasons why you would not want to share information with independent board members. One reason that sharing privileged information with an independent board would be a concern is that you do not trust the board members. To overcome this objection, you should make time to thoroughly check out all potential board members before offering them a position on your board. Once you find trustworthy members, have them review the board constitution (a document that helps set board member expectations) and the code of conduct and ethics. Chapters 7 and 8 discuss the importance of finding trustworthy board members. The board constitution and code of conduct and ethics (covered in

Chapter 10, *How to Develop a Useful Board Const*
board orientation (covered in Chapter 14, *Training B*
show how confidentiality is woven into the boarc
setting process.

Another possible concern with sharing information could simply
be "old business practices." If you want to effectively grow your
company, it is important that the executive team and the board have
an accurate picture of how the company is performing with associated
opportunities and risks. While you do not have to expose your soul
or reveal your innermost secrets, you will be more successful if you
share relevant business information with your board. It breeds trust.
It results in a more objective decision-making process. Keeping all
information close to the vest is an archaic business practice.

A final reason that you may not want to share information is because
there may be something to hide. Under this scenario, you should not
create an independent board. Clean up your internal mess before you
consider creating an independent board.

"We Already Get Good Advice from Consultants, Lawyers, YPO ..."

Consultants, lawyers, accountants, and the like can play an important
role in helping you grow your business. However, these resources
typically focus on solving specific problems. They do not play the
same long-term strategic or policy guidance role that an ongoing
independent board does. If you use an executive coach (they can be
very helpful if you find the right one) who acts as an ongoing advisor,
recognize that he or she only represents one voice, perspective,
or area of expertise. Executive coaches also get involved in both
leadership and management issues (versus focusing mainly on long-
term strategy and policy guidance).

There is another important point to consider. You do not want
consultants and lawyers on your board, as there is the potential for a
conflict of interest. In fact, Sarbanes-Oxley (a law that was enacted
in 2002 as a backlash of the Enron fraud case, among others),

...ifically prohibits company accountants and lawyers from sitting on a public company board. This was done to prevent conflicts of interest. For an independent board to be effective, it must be free of conflicts of interest or misaligned agendas.

If you already use peer learning groups such as Young Presidents Organization (YPO), great! For perspective, YPO is an international organization of presidents and CEOs whose mission is "better leaders through education and idea exchange." YPO, The Executive Committee (TEC) and other peer learning groups are excellent sources of knowledge, advice, and guidance. The only problem with these groups is that there is not enough focus on each specific business. Typically, there are eight to twelve members in a YPO forum group. If you divide meeting time equally among the members, that leaves only about fifteen to thirty minutes per business, each meeting. That simply is not enough time to adequately handle a company's strategy and policy guidance needs. The other point to consider is that these peer learning groups have randomly selected members. This is less effective than an independent board, where specific expertise is recruited that is most relevant to unique business needs.

Does this mean you should resign from your peer learning group(s)? On the contrary, these organizations provide unique learning opportunities and useful advice. An independent board is a great complement to peer learning organizations.

"We Don't Have a Strategic Plan"

Every business has a plan, even though it may not be recognized as such, and not all plans are good. Some plans are in the founder's or business leader's head. That is not the best way to run a business. Problems can occur when the plan is not communicated to employees. What's more, there is a missed opportunity to glean advice on the plan from objective, independent experts. That is a fundamental area where a board can help. As the business evolves, a board can also instill a disciplined (not necessarily cumbersome) planning process.

A strategic plan does not have to be elaborate. It is simply a set of key *choices* (decisions) that leverage a company's competitive advantages to achieve desired future goals (outcomes). Those decisions can be written on one page or many pages. What's important is to write them down. This makes it easier to obtain input from independent experts (i.e., your board), and from your executive team. It also helps communicate the strategic decisions and goals to those that need to know (such as your employees, banker(s), and other business advisors).

Here are a few words of caution: do not wait to start an outside board until you have the "perfect plan" in place. There is no such thing. The plan will evolve because your business and competition will change. Besides, a good board is there to help you improve your plan as the business changes.

4. Get Ready to Take the 5
Steps to Board Success

"By daring to not take the risk of making the new happen, management takes by default, the greater risk of being surprised by what will happen."

— **Peter F. Drucker, one of the world's most influential writers on organizational management**

4. Get Ready to Take the 5 Steps to Board Success

Are You Ready to Win More and Lose Less?

One of the first questions you need to ask is "are you personally ready for an independent board?" The success of a board *depends a lot on you*; a positive attitude is essential.

Are you interested in being more successful? The answer to this question is obvious. However, as you peel back the onion, there are additional questions you should ask to determine if you are ready. For example, are you willing to make the time to find and recruit the right board team? Are you willing to challenge your own leadership practices and focus on the few things that can make the most difference in propelling your business forward? Are you willing to be disciplined to think through and properly prepare so that you have effective board meetings? Are you confident enough to listen to and act upon the board's good advice? Are you willing to be held accountable and make the tough calls, once the harsh reality is presented to you? It is important to note that a peak-performing board should operate based upon facts versus emotion. If you have no intention to listen to or act upon a board's objective advice (including dissenting points of view), then you are not ready for an independent board.

Is Your Business Ready?

Once you are mentally prepared, there are a few business practices that, while not essential, would be helpful to put in place before you create an independent board. First, you should consider having some form of a written plan. Second, it would be helpful to have at least the rudiments of an executive (management) team in place. These two areas are discussed in more detail below.

Written Plan. You will get more out of your board if you can share a written strategic plan with them. The plan does not have to be elaborate. There are many outstanding strategic plans that are documented on only a few pages. What counts is the quality of the thinking that goes into your strategic choices.

Unfortunately, strategic planning is often misunderstood. Consequently, it is misused or not used. Strategic planning is simply a decision process that helps you succeed. It provides a framework for making decisions (choices) of what to include and what to *exclude*. Every business has to consider the fact that change is inevitable. Strategic planning proactively helps a business control its future destiny. It does this by identifying options to get to a future state then prioritizing which options (decisions) are best to achieve that future desired state.

Benefits of a Strategic Plan

A good strategic plan:

- Maps a better course to take the company from its current to its future desired state;
- Clarifies an organization's purpose, mission, strategies, goals, measures, and the like. As such, it ensures that key leaders are all using the same script. It provides alignment throughout the company;
- Enables a company to set and communicate priorities, responsibilities, and measures. It helps monitor success (or failure) and areas where improvement is needed.
- Helps a company work more effectively and efficiently so that it grows, earns more profit, and beats the competition.

What Could Be Included

If you do not have a written plan, you and your executive team have probably already thought through some of the key elements of a good plan.

This book is not intended to guide you in "how to" write a detailed strategic plan. However, you should consider addressing the following topics and related questions for your plan.

❖ **Purpose**—Defines the fundamental reason the company exists. It should guide the company for decades. It is similar to a star, out there on the horizon always guiding and pulling the company towards its destiny. It should inspire change and progress.

❖ **Mission**—A bold, compelling audacious goal that defines a specific destiny. It should fit within a five to ten year time horizon. Too many company mission statements are vague and confusing. The mission needs to be focused, specific, understandable, and time bound. It should be consistent with the purpose. The purpose and mission are different but they work together. The mission is the specific mountain you are crossing. All of your energy and focus are directed towards the mountain you are climbing and how best to succeed. The purpose is the star, off in the distance that guides you while crossing the specific mountain.

❖ **Core Values** – The standards or principles of which a company adheres to, or by which it operates. Values are linked to the relationships the company has with customers, employees, shareholders, suppliers, the community, and other stakeholders. Ask: "What are the key values or fundamental truths under which the company will consistently and universally operate?"

❖ **Strengths/Advantages** – What are the company's strengths or advantages (as viewed from the customer's perspective)? Strengths (advantages) tend to be internally focused and are related to prior resource, structural, and organizational choices. Which advantages are most important? Can the company build upon them? If so, what is the investment required to do so? Will it be worth the projected return on the effort?

❖ **Weaknesses/Limitations** – What are the company's weaknesses (in order of magnitude)? Similar to strengths noted above, these tend to be related to prior internal resource, structural, or organizational choices. Which limitations are most detrimental? Can the company eliminate or reduce them? If so, what is the investment required to minimize them? Will it be worth the projected return on the effort?

❖ **Opportunities** – What are the company's opportunities (in order of magnitude)? Opportunities tend to be external factors triggered by the economy, government regulations, competition, structural changes within the company's industry, and the like. Which opportunities are most lucrative? Can the company exploit them? If so, what is the investment required to do so? Will it be worth the projected return on the effort?

❖ **Threats** – What are the key threats facing the company (in order of magnitude)? Similar to opportunities noted above, these tend to be external factors. Which threats are most detrimental? Can the company avoid them? If so, what is the investment required to avoid them? Will it be worth the projected return on the effort?

❖ **Unique Business Model (UBM)**—Starting with the strengths (advantages) analysis noted above, identify a concentrated advantage (one that is high leverage) that the company does better than anyone else, is unique and meaningful to customers, and is defendable against competition. In essence, the company wants to leverage the *unique* part of the business that gives it a reason to win (beat the competition). It is important to look at the company's UBM from the customer's perspective. Ask: "What are the most meaningful benefits the company can offer current and prospective customers?... Why do customers uniquely buy from the company?... Can the company provide better customer value than the competition?" Lastly, the UBM should incorporate barriers-to-entry that make it harder for the competition to compete.

❖ **Team Strength**—Does the company have the right team to compete effectively? Is the team working on the right activities to achieve the company's key long-term goals?

If not, how can the company improve the team? What will the company need to invest to improve the team? Will it be worth the projected return on the investment?

❖ **Objectives, Goals, and Measurements**—Are the employees working against the right long-term objectives and goals? If not, how can the company realign the team so that it is collectively focused on the right activities? What are the few key milestones that describe future success? Can the company measure them? Are they the right measures? Are the measures reliable and useful? Are they shared with the right stakeholders and at the right frequency?

The first time you develop a written plan, you may want to use the help of an independent consultant, executive coach or planning group. A good resource can help facilitate the strategic planning process. YPO and other peer learning organizations are resources to consider. Ask business leaders who run successful businesses how they approach strategic planning. Check with your local business schools or chamber of commerce. They may know good independent strategic planning consultants or resources that can help you with your plan. You may also want to see the "strategy" section located within the *Suggested Reading* resources at the end of this book for additional information and resources.

Executive Team. Most small to midsize businesses can benefit from an executive (management) team. This does not have to be a large, bureaucratic team. Oftentimes, simple is better. If you develop an executive team, it is a good idea to have key responsibilities assigned and understood among members. Role clarity and alignment are important to achieve top performance.

If you do not have an executive team in place, you may want to consider creating one before you recruit a board. Otherwise, you may waste time and money. This team will provide traction to ensure the board's advice is acted upon. It will also help create and implement the strategic plan.

The 5 Steps: An Overview

Once you are mentally prepared, a written strategic plan and the executive team are in place, you are ready to create an independent board (or improve an existing board). As shown in the following diagram, there are five "right" steps to create or run a successful independent board of directors or advisors.

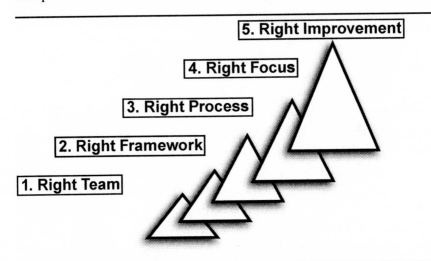

These 5 Steps represent simple building blocks. They will enable you to create or lead a peak-performing board. The 5 Steps are integrally linked. They build upon each other. If executed well, they will lead to greater long-term success, including higher profits, and improved shareholder value.

5 Right Steps Positively Affect Long-Term Results

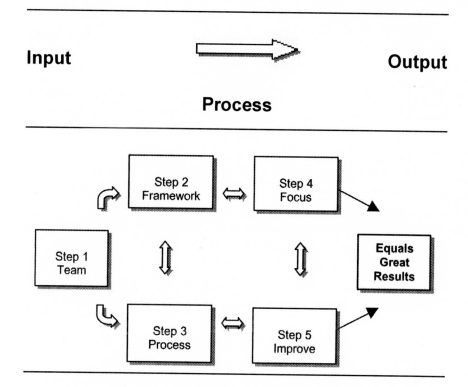

To aid in comprehension and improve take-away value, this book is grouped into sections. Five of the sections correlate with the 5 Steps necessary for peak board performance. The 5 Steps are analogous to the ingredients that successful professional sports teams possess.

The first step (Right Team) is the all-important "draft," or recruiting, of key board members. It is comparable to having the right coach and players on a professional sports team. Obtaining great board members is just as critical. Just like in professional sports, identifying and recruiting a board team must be done right; otherwise, the board will not be successful.

The second step (Right Framework), is similar to a professional sports team's need for clear guidelines, ample salaries, along with the proper equipment and playing field to execute their skills. Similarly, a board should be set up with the proper framework. It should have a clear board constitution (a written document that sets expectations). Fair compensation, good insurance (to protect members), and appropriate term limits are other important elements of the board's framework.

Step 3, the Right Process, (operationally, doing things right), is comparable to a sports team having a disciplined training and practice regimen, and the right preparation. From a board perspective, this means properly orienting new board members. It also means running effective meetings. There are chapters within Step 3 that contain tools and techniques for training board members and running highly productive board meetings. A key goal of establishing the right processes is to have open communication, so that high trust and candor occurs among board members.

Step 4, the Right Focus (strategically, doing the right things), is comparable to a sports team having the right strategy and plays to enable it to win. From a business perspective, it means focusing on the highest leverage opportunities facing the business and prudently acting upon those opportunities. In this step, the 15 Key Strategic Questions every business should answer will be revealed. They will guide a business to the right "plays." There is also a chapter on the art of listening, a key requirement for effectively leading a board.

Step 5 (Right Improvement), is similar to using statistics and other measures of performance to improve a professional sports team. Recording the right metrics is necessary to determine current performance so that purposeful improvement can occur. Similarly, evaluating individual board member and overall board performance is an important path towards higher performance. Unfortunately, board evaluations are rarely utilized in small to midsize businesses. Step 5 provides easy-to-use board performance evaluation tools. It also discusses how those evaluations can be used to improve the board.

As you turn the remaining pages, you will be on your journey; ascending towards greater success. Let's begin with Step 1 (Right Team).

(Step 1)
THE RIGHT BOARD TEAM

1. Right Team

This section covers the all-important first step of building the right team. The team leader is one of the most critical members. In most businesses, that leader is the CEO. Thus, it begins with a chapter that will review what an effective CEO does. The next chapter will provide a similar review but from the board member's perspective. Chapters on identifying and recruiting great board members will conclude Step 1.

5. How the CEO Can Maximize Board Effectiveness

"Leadership is not just about humility and modesty. It is equally about ferocious resolve, an almost stoic determination to do whatever needs to be done to make the company great."

—Jim Collins, national bestselling business author and a student of enduring companies

5. How the CEO Can Maximize Board Effectiveness

Discussed below are behaviors, activities, and responsibilities that a leader (typically the CEO) of a small to midsize business should exhibit to maximize the long-term results of the business and the effectiveness of the board. Listed first are five important overall business criteria that a successful CEO should demonstrate. The remaining CEO behaviors, activities, and responsibilities are specific to effectively leading the board.

Five Important Overall Business Criteria

1. Maximizes Long-Term Shareholder Value — The CEO's ultimate responsibility is to *maximize long-term shareholder value.* In closely held small or midsize companies, a shareholder is often the CEO, a family member, an outside investor, or a member of the senior management team. Regardless, the CEO should act as the servant leader. He or she is entrusted as the steward for all of the owners and their long-term financial interests in the business.

2. Develops the Right Strategic Plan — An essential element of CEO leadership is to ensure the company is playing in the right game and has the right game plan to win (i.e., the right strategic plan). The CEO (with his or her executive team and input from the board) develops the strategic plan with a compelling purpose, clear mission, concrete long-term goals, specific steps to achieve those goals, and appropriate measures and accountabilities.

The CEO makes sure the business is competing in a game in which it has some control over the outcomes and, has a calculated chance to win. Most important, the strategic plan should identify the right business model (preferably unique) and competitive advantages for the business. The CEO should leverage those advantages for sustained growth.

The CEO ensures that the plan does not sit on a shelf, in a folder, or in a computer. Most successful businesses have an evolving game plan and that's OK. Walt Disney said it well: *"Always remember that this whole thing started with a mouse."* The CEO adjusts the plan as the business evolves.

3. Picks the Right Team — The CEO picks the right executive team that implements the plan. He or she ensures that *all* players are high caliber, the team has the full range of skills to compete effectively, (with minimal gaps), they are in the right positions, and the performance of the team remains high.

4. Establishes the Right Culture — The CEO establishes the appropriate culture for the company. Values are built into a company in part by what the CEO does, not what he or she says. Most highly effective business leaders have a passion to win, which is shown through a consistent, tenacious effort. Complacency is not an option.

Another way the CEO effectively establishes a winning culture is by confronting issues head-on. General Colin Powell, the secretary of state under President George W. Bush, put together a *Leadership Primer, a Collection of Lessons for Leaders.* His first lesson is captured in this quote by him: *"Being responsible sometimes means pissing people off."* He elaborates under this lesson that: *"Good leadership involves responsibility to the welfare of the group, which means that some people will get angry at your actions and decisions. It's inevitable if you're honorable. Trying to get everyone to like you is a sign of mediocrity: you'll avoid the tough decisions, you'll avoid confronting the people who need to be confronted, and you'll avoid offering differential rewards based on differential performance because some people might get upset."* It is up to the CEO to make the right calls, even if from time to time they "piss some people off." This element of leadership is one of the most effective ways to create the right culture for a business.

5. Establishes Accountability — The CEO develops a measurement system to evaluate progress versus the strategic plan. Just as important, the leader accepts personal accountability to the company's plan. He or she pursues the plan's goals with rigor and discipline.

Board-Specific Criteria

The foregoing are important behaviors, activities, and responsibilities a CEO should demonstrate in order to maximize overall business effectiveness. Following are CEO behaviors, activities, and responsibilities that relate more specifically to the board.

Leads Board Effectiveness — In a closely held (private) business, the CEO is typically the board chair. The board chair is responsible for leading the board and maximizing its effectiveness. Legally, the shareholders elect the board and the board elects the officers. Practically, in a private business, the CEO picks the board team.

To be successful, the CEO must pick the right board team of experts. He or she must establish a culture of high trust. The CEO should ensure that board members understand their roles. Further, as board chair, the CEO has the opportunity to reinforce proper board expectations during every board meeting and every board member encounter.

On a related point, since all companies undergo change over time, the CEO (and the board) must periodically review its effectiveness. As needs arise, the CEO (and board) should ensure that the board has the right team to help the business accomplish its long-term goals.

Effectively Communicates with the Board — In the dual roles of board chair and CEO, the CEO must develop a trusting communications approach to share what is going on in the company and in the market. The CEO ensures that all board members are effectively informed. All peak-performing boards have one thing in common: the CEO promptly and appropriately keeps the board apprised of developments in the business. He or she facilitates open and ongoing communication with the board before, during, and outside of formal board meetings.

The CEO reports to the board on the activities and the performance of his or her direct reports, and how the business is doing versus plan. Simple and high-level comparison charts should be used to report on key metrics. These metrics should be updated and shared before every board meeting (it is a good idea to include these in the board report).

Creates a Trusting Board Environment — The CEO creates an atmosphere or climate of trust and truth where every board member feels comfortable speaking his or her mind. The CEO encourages the board to challenge the executive team—particularly when the business is performing *well*. Groupthink should be minimized. A good CEO works hard to ensure that individual points of view are welcome.

Asks, Listens, and then Acts upon Board Advice, as Appropriate — The CEO is responsible for constantly asking the board members: *"What do you think?"* Just as important, the CEO is responsible for listening to the board and acting upon their good advice, as appropriate.

While independent board members bring valuable expertise and experience, they are not as close to all of the business issues as is the executive (or management) team. In addition, it is common to obtain conflicting advice from board members, and that is OK. Not all board advice is good, relevant, or appropriate, but it should be listened to, discussed, and considered. Thus, the CEO and the executive team often have to make final decisions on a viable course of action for a business after considering input from the board.

6. What Makes Great Board Members?

"When two people in business always agree, one of them is not necessary."

—William Wrigley, Jr., founder of Wrigley's chewing gum

6. What Makes Great Board Members?

Listed below is a series of important attributes that describe great board members. By design, these attributes are universal. They apply to all great board members, regardless of the size or type of business or board. A thorough understanding of these attributes will help in identifying great board candidates, which is the subject of the next chapter. If a great board candidate can be accurately defined, it is much easier to find and recruit the right board members.

Possess High Integrity

This attribute is paramount. It speaks for itself. Quality board members do not have conflicts of interest or other unethical issues. They have no incentive for personal gain at the expense of the company. On the contrary, they have a consistent track record of high-integrity behavior as evidenced through past actions. They will take on the "duties of care" without hesitation.

A high-integrity board member can reduce a company's potential exposure to unethical issues. This is important in a post-Enron world.

Share Expertise

Each board member is on the board because he or she has a high level of a specific expertise that the company needs in order to accomplish its long-term goals. Great board members unselfishly share that expertise with the company and other board members in an appropriate manner.

Act Responsibly

Great board members act responsibly. They do not become involved in a board position as a perk or reward for deeds done well elsewhere. They understand that a board position is not a trophy. Instead, they view it as a responsibility to perform duties in good faith and for the best long-term interests of the shareholders and the company.

Hold Confidences

It is essential that all board members keep what is discussed in the board meetings confidential. Absolutely nothing confidential in nature should be discussed with anyone outside of the boardroom.

Any breach of confidence is immediate grounds for dismissal. Possible legal action may also be warranted, contingent upon the severity of the breach. There are no ifs, ands, or buts. If there is any doubt in a board member's mind that something may or may not be confidential, they should err on the conservative side.

Good Judgment

Fundamentally, every great board member should possess good judgment. You are entrusting the company's future in the hands of a few individuals. You want people on your board team who consistently make good, well-reasoned, and preferably fact-based decisions.

Focus on Long-Term Strategy and Policy

Great board members know how to stay focused on a strategic level. They do not try to lead or manage the day-to-day business. That's the role of the CEO and his or her executive team.

Great board members challenge the business leaders. They ask questions to learn if the CEO has recruited the right team. They ensure that the CEO and the executive team have a good strategic plan... that the purpose and mission are compelling... that the future opportunities are good bets... that the company is constantly stretching its boundaries and possibilities.

If the CEO cannot develop a good plan, then the board needs to go back and help pick the right CEO (especially if it is a broadly held public company board).

If the situation involves a closely held company, the board should provide the appropriate performance feedback to the CEO. Board members should reconsider if they want to be on the board if the CEO does not take the feedback to heart. The other option is to convince the owner/CEO that they should hire a professional manager (president, COO or CEO). A great board does this in a tactful way that helps the CEO understand why this is necessary.

Help Invent

This is where a diverse board of experts often shows its greatest strength. Great board members use their expertise to bring fresh ideas and new points of view for the CEO and executive team to consider. They are confident enough to share out-of-the-box ideas with the company. They challenge boundaries, explore new possibilities, find creative solutions, and help the company invent. They do this without wearing rose-colored glasses.

Participate

Great board members are punctual and fully prepared for every meeting. They want to attend all meetings (unless there is a true emergency). Of note, attendance should be mandatory.

Great board members are readily accessible and do work between meetings. They initiate conversation with the CEO and the company outside of official board meetings, as appropriate.

Open participation, both by listening and through verbal communication, is an utter necessity in a board meeting. Great board members participate in a balanced manner. While they should share their own point of view and expertise, they should not monopolize meeting time. They recognize that there are other board experts on the team who bring valuable advice and skills to the table (albeit from a different perspective). If there are differences in opinion, they acknowledge and respect those differences.

Great board members also have the confidence to say "I don't know." They do not take a "hip shooter" approach just to show participation. They recognize that no one has all of the answers.

Great board members maintain active participation over the years. They do not become "stale." Their energy and enthusiasm remain high. Otherwise, the board member should opt out. Of note, periodic performance reviews help ensure consistent, high-level board member performance.

Objectively Communicate

Great board members offer objective, honest advice. They do not have hidden agendas or share personal biases. A straightforward, apolitical approach is best. Great board members are outspoken. They speak their mind. They express a point of view firmly but not harshly. This is done without alienating other board members.

Great board members probe to understand truth. They ask good, pointed questions with the goal to help the business and to support the long-term interests of the shareholders.

Passionate

Great board members are passionate about the business. They are not passive during board meetings. Great board members demonstrate a proficient and solid understanding of the business, markets, competitive landscape, and the like. They show initiative by constantly looking for ways to improve the business. A good sign of commitment is sometimes evidenced when board members naturally speak in terms of "our" company or "we" should do this.

Team Players

It takes new employees about three to six months to fit into a company. Board members only have a handful of days per year to develop positive working relationships with the other members and management. Thus, it is important to find board members who have the right chemistry and are good team players.

Great board members work well with the board team. They do this, in part, by respecting other members' opinions and by not dominating meeting air time. They recognize what skills and expertise other board members possess (having a board with non-overlapping skills is recommended). They defer to that expertise, as appropriate. Listening to and building upon suggestions is another way board members demonstrate that they are team players.

Identify and Manage Risks

The ability to identify and manage risks is a key role for great board members. Once risks are known, the board helps the company make prudent choices with respect to minimizing those risks. However, a board member should not continually say the sky is falling, *unless it really is falling—then he or she should be very vocal.* This is particularly true with entrepreneurial ventures that grow at fast rates and experience rapid changes.

Identify What's Missing

Great board members have the ability to see beyond the obvious and identify what is missing. Many board members can reveal how to improve what is proposed or identify what has gone wrong. Not many board members are able to see what is not there.

Network

Great board members help the CEO network. Examples of networking include new business leads, sources of employee talent, better suppliers, and the like. Each board member should significantly expand the company's connections to useful resources that can help build the business. Great board members actively use their networks to help the company, as appropriate.

Ensure Accountability

The CEO should be held accountable for his or her decisions and actions. Great board members recognize this. They point out what is right about a strategic plan to help preserve it. Conversely, they point out what is wrong with the plan to help improve it. Of note, the strategic plan (not necessarily the strategy) is usually out of date the day after it is written. Competition does not sit still, nor do technology, government, capital markets, and other external environmental forces that impact the business. Great board members keep the strategic plan alive. They ensure it evolves, as appropriate.

Great board members ensure accountability when times are bad and when times are good. As soon as the business appears to be doing well—*watch out!* That is the time to be concerned. It is easy for any business to become complacent and hide when business appears to be going well. Great board members keep pushing—*especially when times are good.* They consistently raise the bar of expectations. This helps to ensure excellent long-term results.

Help with Succession/Exit

In public companies, board members help pick the executive officers of the company, including the CEO. This occurs infrequently. Therefore, board members do not get a lot of practice with this important task. What's more, it is a *difficult* task.

In Limited Liability Corporations (LLC) and small to midsize, private companies, a succession plan may be a more difficult issue to bring up in a board meeting. However, it should be periodically discussed. All businesses should have a succession plan that is reviewed annually. The board can play an invaluable role with succession planning.

A tactful way to bring up succession planning is to ask the following innocent yet important question: "What would happen if a very unfortunate event occurred and the CEO suddenly and unexpectedly was hit by a bus and passed away or was severely disabled?"

The board should insist that a succession plan be in place. Just as important, it should be prepared to help, if the succession plan needs to be implemented. One approach is to include in the annual strategic plan, an answer to the innocent question noted above. It would be beneficial to the business and board to have a short list of potential replacement candidates if the CEO were to unexpectedly leave the business.

Related to succession is the need for an exit plan. The executive team should have a point of view on the company's potential exit strategy. If it is a family business, is the goal to pass it on to the next generation? In a non-family business, is the plan to sell the business? The board can be instrumental in transitioning a business from one owner or leader to another.

7. Keys to Identifying Great Board Members

"When you reach for the stars, you may not get one, but you won't come up with a handful of mud either."

—Leo Burnett, founder of Leo Burnett Company, a leading advertising agency. Leo Burnett Company created the Marlboro Man, Tony the Tiger, the Jolly Green Giant, and other enduring advertising characters.

7. Keys to Identifying Great Board Members

Look for the Right Experts

If you want a peak-performing board, you need to identify the right board experts. This is critical. It is the essence of Step 1 (Right Team). It is the key input in the board effectiveness equation. The engineer's old saying of "garbage in, garbage out" is very revealing. When considering board members, it should be reworded to "greatness in, greatness out." This is the approach you must take when scouting for your board members. Overall, you want to find people who have a genuine high-level competency in and passion for their specific area of expertise.

Your search will require a manageable but not insignificant up-front investment of time. As another old saying goes: "You get out of it what you put into it." However, making the time to find the best board experts for your business will pay big dividends. This chapter will help you identify what to look for. The next chapter will cover practical and efficient ways to find great board members.

Look for a Team of Experts

A balanced team with diversity in expertise is very important to creating an effective board. Just like any successful sports team, you do not want all of your players with the same skills, talents, and perspectives. Imagine a baseball team with only outstanding pitchers and poor-performing catchers, fielders, or hitters. It would not be very effective. However, a sports team with great pitchers and strong fielders, hitters, and the like is a recipe for success. Having a balanced team of experts applies to business boards.

Another important factor with respect to variety is to find expertise that is relevant to your business: marketing, financial, technological, product development, operational, or whatever your needs may be.

Before recruiting potential members, it is a good idea to identify the key long-term issues or challenges facing your business. Having people on your board who have already experienced the big issues you are facing or will face is invaluable. The flattening of your learning curve and related time savings can translate into meaningful bottom-line results. For example, if you have aggressive growth plans, recruit a board member who has had experience leading a high-growth company. If you are in the high-tech market, it would be wise to find a board member who has a solid technology background. Likewise, if you have ongoing and troublesome union labor issues, finding a candidate who has navigated through difficult union negotiations could be very beneficial to you. And family businesses have their own special needs, as do start-up companies. The point is, find the expertise that will help the company win.

Look for Truth and Objectivity

Truth is the *absolute essential ingredient* you want from every board member. You want board members who are not afraid to tell you what they really think. They should be free from conflicts in speaking the truth. Look for board members who are not afraid to tell you that you are wrong. They need to be able to speak up and say, "The emperor has no clothes." Hopefully, board members will use tact when they speak, since many business leaders are overachievers and may find criticism hard to swallow.

Business environments, competitive circumstances, and other external or internal factors can change business prospects very quickly. Sometimes the leadership team is marching down the wrong path and does not realize it. You need board members who are in touch with real business world conditions. Board members should be confident. They should be capable of telling you that the world is not the same. They need to have courage in their convictions. They need to be able to challenge your plans and assumptions. They need to illuminate the harsh realities, so that the business deals with a realistic picture.

You do not want "rubber stamp" CYA (cover-your-butt) types. Boards made up of friends or other "management pleasers" are unhealthy for any business. Thus, it is essential that you do not recruit a bunch of your friends for your board. If you consider a friend, he or she must be exceptional. Otherwise, you can jeopardize your friendship, the board's effectiveness, or both. Besides, it's easier to find good board members than it is to find good friends.

Good board members should be free to make inquiries into policy and strategy issues. They should feel free to share a dissenting point of view, if appropriate.

Independent board members should exercise independent judgment. You do not want suppliers, consultants, or key customers on your board. Doing so could compromise independence. It could put both parties in a potential conflict-of-interest dilemma.

Lastly, you want board members who can keep the truth held within the confines of your board meetings. You will be sharing a lot of highly confidential business and personal information. You want board members who can keep confidences.

Look for Wisdom

Avoid "celebrity" directors. To quote Erma Bombeck: *"Don't confuse fame with success. Madonna is one; Helen Keller is the other."* Look for people who have a passion to solve strategic problems, have a thirst to learn, and are willing to share their knowledge and expertise.

Search for wise, independent-minded people. Seek out street-smart, pragmatic thinkers. Avoid theoreticians who do not have a real-world, practical business perspective. On the other hand, you may want a few seasoned CEOs on your board team. There is a real advantage in having people on your board who have "walked a mile or two in your moccasins."

Look for Commitment

To be effective, all board members must be truly engaged in your business. They should be willing to learn your business in enough depth so that they are not "hip shooters." Each board member needs to be prepared and attend *every* meeting. They also need to help out between meetings. Thus, it goes without saying that you need to find people who can commit their time to your board.

Another point to consider on board member commitment is that you want to ensure that the member's agenda is aligned with the business's agenda. There should be no personal inconsistencies with the board's purpose. Developing a board constitution and reviewing it with prospective board members before they are given an offer to join will help ensure alignment.

A final point to note on board member commitment is that you want board members who will maintain their commitment over the years. You do not want them to become stale. Their energy and enthusiasm should remain high. Periodic performance reviews will help ensure consistent, high-level board member performance.

Look for Networks

One of the benefits of a board is that it can significantly expand the company's network. As such, you should look for candidates with broad and influential connections. Just as important, the contacts should respect the candidate so that a connection can be used effectively. Knowing someone is very different than having a meaningful relationship where the real doors get opened.

Build Upon Strengths

It may seem that the most important board members to recruit are ones who complement your weaknesses. That is important; however, do not discount building upon your strengths. For example, if your company is good at innovation, make sure you recruit a board expert who has demonstrated success with innovation, who can contribute to and amplify this competency. Likewise, if your company is strong at operational efficiencies (i.e. you are a low-cost producer), you will want a board member on your team who is a demonstrated black belt in operational excellence.

Look to Complement Weaknesses

An effective board team also means recruiting board members who complement the executive teams' professional *weaknesses.* Strengths often mirror weaknesses. Unfortunately, sometimes we are blind to those weaknesses. It is important to understand your company's professional weaknesses. Recruit board members who complement those weaker areas. For example, if the CEO is a big-picture marketing and sales person who is not very interested in thinking through the details (tactics), make sure you have a board member who understands the necessity of *linking the details and processes of your business to the big picture. There is a graveyard filled with former businesses that stumbled because senior management overlooked the important integration and cross-fertilization of strategy with tactics.*

Look for Prior Board Experience

Generally, the more you do something, the more proficient you become at it. Being a board member is no different. Thus, it is prudent to recruit one or two board members who have had prior board experience (assuming that experience was effective).

Recruiting a few experienced board veterans can be especially helpful when you are creating a new board. They can play an important mentoring role to the less experienced members.

Statutory boards should seek at least one member with financial expertise. If you are contemplating an IPO or are involved with a broadly traded public company, it is a requirement of Sarbanes-Oxley to have financial audit expertise represented on the board. For these situations, ideally, you should seek someone with public company audit experience from a quality accounting firm. People with this background have typically stuck there noses into a number of different businesses from the financial side and are generally familiar with GAAP. This experience gives them an edge in knowing the right questions to ask and where the issues are with respect to public company financial requirements.

Another specific prior board experience you may want to look for is that of board chair. This will be especially important if the CEO does not serve as the chair. The board chair is an important role. Experience will improve effectiveness.

Here is a word of caution: If you recruit board members with prior board experience, make sure that experience is appropriate for your board situation. In the words of Lisa FitzGibbon, president of the Work Resource Center, on whose board the author participated, "I've hit some speed bumps with board members who have been on other boards but those boards micromanaged or rubber-stamped or operated in some other dysfunctional way. I then had to expend effort to re-socialize them."

Avoid Tactical Advisors

Do not have your tactical business advisors on your board. It is strongly suggested that you *do not* use your accountants, lawyers, or other tactical business advisors for your board. First of all, you already have them on your business team to help with day-to-day issues. Second, there is always the *potential* for a conflict of interest (they may seek more of your business; possibly for the wrong reasons). Thus, it is better to eliminate a potential conflict of interest dilemma altogether.

Look for Fit

Ultimately, you need board members with whom you can work well, and who can work well with other members of your board team. That does not mean they should be your friends. To the contrary, as previously mentioned, friends can be problematic. What you do want is good chemistry among all board members. This can be difficult to specify and thus, is harder to identify. So how do you know if the chemistry is right? This is a gut-level decision—"you will know it when you feel it."

Summary of What to Avoid

You now have a framework of what peak-performing board members look like. While it may appear redundant, since selecting the right experts is so important, it may be helpful to review board members from an opposite perspective; what to avoid. To that end, below is a brief list of what you should avoid when considering board members.

- ❖ **Unethical** — It does not matter how "good" a person may be from an expertise perspective; you do not want anyone on your board who is in the least bit dishonest or unethical. Reference checking and the "tummy test" (using your gut and intuition) are good ways to minimize the chance that an unethical person ends up on your board.

- ❖ **Poor Judgment** — Avoid people who have poor judgment. This does not mean you should eliminate people who have made mistakes. On the contrary, many of the best board candidates have learned through their mistakes. Peel back the onion and find out if the mistakes were a result of poor judgment or other circumstances beyond the person's reasonable control.

- ❖ **Conflicted** — You do not want anyone on your board who has an agenda that is different from the shareholders' or the company's agenda. Different agendas can be problematic, as they often lead to unhealthy friction or, even worse, bad decisions, and potentially fraud and/or liability consequences.

- ❖ **Expertise Redundancy** — You do not want duplicate board members who possess the same expertise. They will add little value to the board.

- ❖ **Risk Averse** — You do not want board members who are extremely risk averse. However, you do want board members who are calculated risk takers. Prudent risk takers will expand your perspectives. They will help you explore new possibilities. Your business often reflects the makeup of your board. If you do not want to accept the status quo, then avoid ultra-conservative people who are too afraid to venture, stretch, learn, grow, or invent.

❖ **Poor Team Players**—Avoid poor team players. It is important that you have a professional working relationship with *all* of your board members. *The chemistry among the members must be good.* Otherwise, you may experience excessive stress. More important, the board's performance will suffer. You should be able to find board candidates who have the right qualities which you desire and who are good team players.

❖ **Know-It-Alls** — Avoid people who think they know everything. People who think they have all of the answers have no place on a peak-performing board. On a related point, avoid candidates who have to compete with others to show how smart they are.

❖ **Theoretical Thinkers**—Avoid overly theoretical thinkers. Business is common sense. Theory may be good in the classroom, but it has little value in a boardroom unless it is tempered with real-world experience or exceptional expertise.

❖ **Status Seekers**—Avoid people who are seeking a board position as a status symbol. You want board members who understand that they are accepting a *responsibility* to serve on your board, not a status position or reward.

❖ **Uncommitted** — Avoid people who cannot guarantee you a genuine commitment in time and energy to your board.

❖ **Friends and Family**—Avoid family and friends. A board's true effectiveness stems from harnessing the strategic advice and wisdom of objective *independent experts*. Cluttering a board with friends and family will significantly hinder a board's effectiveness.

❖ **Accountants, Lawyers, Financial Advisors, and the Like** — You already have these day-to-day advisors on your team. Do not increase the chances that a conflict of interest could occur.

❖ **Customers and Suppliers** — Avoid an unnecessary possibility for a conflict of interest. Customers and suppliers interests' may not be aligned with shareholders'.

❖ **Executive Team** — Avoid cluttering a board with inside members from the executive team. You can (and should) establish a separate executive team to run the day-to-day business. Both the board and the executive team deal with strategy and policy. However, the board should not be bogged down with short-term tactics. Besides, every board seat that is occupied by an inside member takes away an independent expert (outside) board seat.

8. How to Recruit and Retain Peak-Performing Board Members

"The heights by great men reached and kept,
Were not attained by sudden flight,
But they, while their companions slept,
Were toiling upward in the night."

—Henry Wadsworth Longfellow, one of the best-loved American poets

8. How to Recruit and Retain Peak-Performing Board Members

We have now come to the important task of pulling together the right board team. As already mentioned, if you want a successful board, you will need to invest time during Step 1 to define, find, and recruit the best board members you can. Contained herein are tips that should speed up your search process and more importantly, help you do it right the first time. The first suggestion is straightforward— take time to define the expertise you desire. You should spend no less time defining a new board expert than the time you would spend defining the role of one of your top employees. In fact, the process should be similar.

A Clear Picture: The Written Board Search Description

Chapters 6 and 7 covered an important part of Step 1 (describing what makes great board members and keys to identifying them). We are now going to package that understanding into a tool: a working document to increase the odds that the right team is recruited for your board. In the long run, it is more cost effective and easier to do it right the first time. Thus, clearly defining what the "right expertise" looks like in a simple document is essential. No one likes to suffer disappointments and poor performance later. If you take a "ready, fire, aim" approach, you will likely end up wasting more time "fixing" the business and replacing poor-performing board members. Better to take time and do your homework up front.

A written Board Search Description is recommended. This is related to a job description, but is specific to the board role. A good example is provided in Appendix 1. Portions of that example are shown in Exhibits 1a, 1b, and 1c, which follow in this chapter. As you can see in Exhibit 1a below, the "need" section of the Board Search Description, provides a clear picture of what kind of board expert Peak-Performance seeks to bring onto the board team. Of note, you should adapt this Board Search Description example to accommodate your specific board and business needs.

Exhibit 1a. Board Search Description: "Need" Section Example

---

*Peak-Performance, Inc.**
Board Search Description
(Created November, 2004)

Our Need

- *Peak-Performance's board has been an invaluable source of independent expertise and advice. Our objectives and mission are challenging and evolving and we are seeking a fourth outside board expert to help our company reach its next level of success. Specifically, the company is contemplating an IPO and afterwards plans to evaluate several complementary business acquisition opportunities.*
- *We recognize the value of a financial executive who has already faced similar challenges to what we expect to confront. Thus, we desire a board candidate who has hands-on experience with acquisitions and/or IPOs. Related expertise in hiring and overseeing investment bankers would be very beneficial.*
- *Familiarity with and working knowledge of Sarbanes-Oxley is a must.*
- *Prior board experience preferred but not essential.*

* Note: Peak-Performance, Inc. is a fictitious company that is used as an example throughout this book. The name Peak-Performance was made up by the author and is not intended to be linked or associated with a real company. Any similarities are purely coincidental.

Select Mission Critical, Independent Expertise

Recall from our definition of a board *("A high-performance select team of mostly independent experts...")* that you want to *select* independent expertise. As you can see in the Peak-Performance "need" example above, the company is seeking a financial expert with acquisitions and IPO experience. You want to draw upon expertise that both reinforces and complements the company's and the CEO's professional strengths and weaknesses. The best way to accomplish this is to take an inventory of the company's and CEO's strengths and weaknesses. Once this is done, think through the strategic needs of the company. The strategic plan should reveal these needs. Ask yourself: What are the most important areas of expertise that will help move the company forward?

From the Peak-Performance example, future growth will best come through acquisitions. An IPO is contemplated to fund those acquisitions. As you consider these specific needs and the current makeup of the Peak-Performance board, it becomes very clear what the mission-critical expertise is that the next board member should possess. Your company may need marketing, operations, sales, technology, or some other critical expertise. Regardless, the most important expertise that the company needs to move forward should be determined and pursued.

Add Expertise in the Right Sequence

Not only should you determine what areas of expertise are most critical for the future success of the company, you should develop a plan to recruit your board experts in an order that makes sense. In the Peak-Performance Board Search Description, there is a section that describes each of the three current independent board members' expertise as follows:

- *Former president of a large and successful competitive firm that was sold (ten years high-growth business expertise in the same industry).*
- *Retired senior pharmaceutical marketing executive (thirty years related customer expertise and currently Chair of a start-up company).*
- *Seasoned operations executive (eighteen years operations expertise in an unrelated but highly reputable business).*

73

The initial two independent members brought invaluable industry and customer expertise to the board. They played an important role in the early stages of the company. Specifically, they helped accelerate industry and customer knowledge, which propelled sales. The industry and customer expertise was complemented by the addition of a third independent board member who possessed outstanding operations expertise. That's because after gaining new customers within the industry, operational excellence was the next key ingredient needed for Peak-Performance's growth. The company's sales success necessitated delivering on promises (operational competencies).

Peak-Performance's board member recruitment sequence continues with the addition of a fourth independent member who will bring the next mission critical area of expertise to the board (financial — acquisitions, IPO and Sarbanes-Oxley knowledge).

The Peak-Performance example reflects a pattern that is familiar to high-growth, start-up companies. Every business has specific strategic needs which vary according to business life cycles and market dynamics. Board members should reinforce key competencies. They should fill knowledge gaps that are determined by the strategic opportunities that the company is pursuing.

Once the mission-critical expertise is defined, it is easier to identify and subsequently recruit the right board member(s).

Select Industry Expertise

Sometimes it is beneficial to have a board member or two on the team with a different industry perspective. However, be careful. You do not want all of your board members from outside of your industry. Expertise related to your business can be invaluable. You should have at least one board member who brings this important knowledge to your company.

Select Genetically Encoded Expertise

When looking for expertise (financial, in the Peak-Performance example), look to see if it is "genetically encoded" (a term used by Jim Collins, author of *Good to Great*) within the individual. Specifically, the candidate should have a naturally high level of the desired expertise.

Select a Balanced Team of Experts

The board should be comprised of a balanced team of experts. A lopsided board that has expertise mostly in one area is not nearly as effective as a balanced board that has a variety of experts.

Use Your Board to Help

Assuming a private company situation, if you already have a good board and are looking for additional experts, you should consider letting your existing board help you recruit new members. After all, they know the job best. Another benefit is that this increases objectivity in the selection process. To make it easy for your board members to identify the right candidates, make sure you have an accurate picture of the kind of board expert(s) that you are seeking. Share that understanding with your existing board. The Board Search Description should satisfy this communication need. As a side point, it is also a good idea to obtain the existing board's buy-in to the Board Search Description. Send your board a draft and discuss it during one of your board meetings. For a public company board, typically there is a nominating or governance committee that is responsible for recruiting new members to the board.

Aggressively Network

Look everywhere. Do not be afraid to go outside of your comfort zone. Recruit at professional associations, seminars and industry conferences such as those put on by *Inc.* magazine. Ask fellow business associates and consultants. Send your Board Search Description to your accounting and law firms.

Network through peer learning groups such as YPO (Young Presidents' Organization), WPO (World Presidents' Organization), YEO (Young Entrepreneurs' Organization), and TEC (The Executive Committee), among others. Do not forget your local chamber of commerce, Rotary Club, or business schools. They typically have active networking circles. Industry trade associations, seminars, and conventions are plausible places to find specific industry expertise for your board.

Another tip is to consider the often-overlooked network of executives who have left competitors or who have retired from industries that you compete in or are related to your business. The Peak-Performance board example has two members with these backgrounds. However, you should be cautious when considering retirees. On the one hand, they possess a wealth of knowledge and wisdom. Plus, they most likely have time to commit to your board. On the other hand, you want to be fairly certain that their expertise is still valid and that they will continue to have a thirst for business (so that they will not become stale). If their passion is to play golf every day during retirement, they may not be a good candidate for your board.

Ask Peers

Ask CEOs and other business leaders, especially ones who are competent or have effective boards. Sometimes they can recommend a great board member. They may even have an outstanding member on their board who could be helpful on your board (as long as the candidate possesses the right expertise and is not stretched too thin). A word of caution: If you serve on another board, you should not offer a position on your board to the CEO of that company. This could violate objectivity. It could also increase the potential for a conflict of interest. Either scenario can be unhealthy for both companies.

Another place to look for potential board members is non-profit boards. If you are on a non-profit board and you know of a board member who has the "right stuff," consider approaching him or her for your board. Additionally, talk with the executive director of the non-profit organization and the chair of their board. Ask if they could recommend strong board candidates that have the mission-critical expertise you are seeking. Provide them with your Board Search Description.

Ask for Recommendations

An effective tip that executive recruiters use to broaden their recruiting network is to ask for candidate recommendations from every person they talk to about a position. This is especially relevant among qualified candidates who are not interested in your board position. People typically associate with like-minded people. Oftentimes, they can make excellent suggestions. Thus, make it a habit to ask everyone you speak with about the board position for their suggestions on additional board candidates. Provide them with extra copies of the Board Search Description.

Seek Administrative Help

Here's another recruiting tip. To assist in your search efforts, have your administrative staff and/or human resource employees be on the lookout for potential candidates. You can direct them to look online, in industry publications, local newspapers and in business publications such as the *Wall Street Journal.*

Consider an Executive Recruiter

If your network sphere is inadequate or you do not have the time to find a great board member yourself, consider using an executive recruiter. Note that there are executive recruiters who specialize in board recruitment. However, they do not work for free. You should understand the total investment in fees *and expenses* before hiring one. If you are going to use a recruiter, it is recommended that you hire one with board recruitment experience.

Look Near and Far

Small to midsize businesses should be able to find some or most of their board members locally or regionally. This will cut down on travel expenses. It will also facilitate more direct contact with board members. This does not mean that you should only look in your local area. There are many great candidates who are located in other parts of the country or world. Be aware, though, that travel expenses will be higher and they can add up. Regardless, the guiding principle should be to obtain the best talent you can find, within reason.

Be Thorough

Interviewing and extensive background and reference checking are essential parts of the board member qualification process. In order to avoid setting up a perceived expectation that an interview will result in an obligation, state this beforehand. It may also be a good idea to explain that multiple candidates will be considered and that the full board must approve every candidate (assuming this is the case). As an aside, it is recommended that at least two and preferably three qualified people (e.g., current board members, the CEO, senior members of the executive team) interview final board candidates. In addition to getting a more informed perspective, it enables the interviewer to set the expectation that before an offer is made, all interviewers must caucus and present to the board their recommendations.

Send the prospect information about your company before the meeting. You may want to include product samples or company brochures. This will help familiarize the board candidate with your company.

Schedule the interview in a comfortable setting, perhaps over lunch in a quiet restaurant. Another option is to conduct the interview at company headquarters. The advantage with this option is that the candidate can see the company and its products firsthand.

During the interview, you should begin with broader questions to determine general board member effectiveness (see Chapter 6 for a review of what makes great board members) and why they would want to serve on your board. Only consider candidates who view the board position as a *responsibility*. You do not want board members who see the position as a reward or honor for prior efforts.

After the broader questions are covered, probe to help you determine the amount and level of expertise (i.e. acquisitions expertise) that the candidate possesses. Your Board Search Description should help you focus your questions in the right areas.

Conduct the interview in a friendly, conversational tone. Similar to interviewing employees, it is important to show interest and to maintain rapport. Avoid questions that elicit a "yes" or "no" response. You will learn more by asking open-ended questions. Use of the "W" questions (what, when, where, who, and why) coupled with "how" fit most board candidate interview situations. The "W" questions are brief and to the point. For example, "What was your role… Why did you make that decision?" The "W" questions elicit detailed answers, obtain more complete information, and save time.

After your questions are asked, it is important to listen for evidence that the candidate would add value to your board. Make sure that you understand what the candidate is saying. If the answers are not clear, seek clarification. You also want to make sure that the answers relate to what you are seeking in a candidate (use the Board Search Description as a guide). Be sure that you have enough information to evaluate the candidate's capabilities and expertise.

Present the Opportunity Accurately

The board candidate interview process should be a two-way street. Each candidate should have ample time to get to know your business, your board, and what they could expect should they be chosen to be a board member. An effective way you can begin educating candidates on the business is to include an overview of your company in the Board Search Description. A good example is provided in Appendix 1 and in Exhibit 1b below. The "our business" section of the Board Search Description provides a clear yet brief overview of the business. If done right, the board candidate should quickly understand the company's past, its current situation, and its future plans.

Below is a checklist of information you may want to include in the "our business" section of your Board Search Description. It is important to objectively portray the company in this description. Otherwise, both the company and the board candidate could be misled. This information should be supplemented with company brochures, purpose, mission, and values statements, a code of conduct and ethics, and other relevant information you have available to share.

Information to Include in the "Our Business" Section of a Board Search Description

➢ Brief history of the company with key transitions
➢ Scope of the current business (number of employees, office locations, sales, etc.)
➢ Type of business (family, private, public, entrepreneurial, professionally managed, etc.)
➢ Customers and markets served (industries, local, domestic, international, etc.)
➢ Products offered, with brief descriptions
➢ Strategic positioning
➢ Company culture and structure
➢ A top-line financial snapshot of the business
➢ Future strategic direction, broadly described (avoid highly confidential plans)

As you can see in the business description in Exhibit 1b, below, the reader has a clear understanding of the company's history, current scope, and future direction. It also sets up the need for a financial board expert. Note: During the early stages of candidate discussions, you should not share highly confidential information (such as your strategic plan). That information can be shared at a later date, if warranted.

Exhibit 1b. Board Search Description: "Business" Section Example

---

Peak-Performance, Inc.
Board Search Description
(Created July, 2004)

<u>*Our Business*</u>

- *A private, closely held company since inception (established in 1987) with headquarters in Cincinnati and sales offices in New York and Philadelphia.*
- *Leading niche player in physician office-based targeted media (see Statement of Purpose document that follows). Created and installed over 80,000 informational displays that reach over 50 million U.S.-based health-conscious consumers each year (see company brochures).*
- *Award-winning company (#23 in* Inc. *magazine's 500 Fastest Growing Private Companies List, Cincinnati Chamber of Commerce, Small Business of the Year).*
- *High organic growth (29 percent average per year) with approximately $31 million in sales and seventy-five employees.*
- *Results-oriented, entrepreneurial culture that lives by its principles (see attached Statement of Purpose).*
- *Excellent customer satisfaction and repeat business. Eleven of the top twenty pharmaceutical companies are clients (all are* Fortune 500 *companies). Seven have been customers for over eight years.*
- *Strong balance sheet and fourteen-year track record of profitability. Equity is internally owned.*
- *Balanced and experienced management team in all key functional areas, but no acquisitions or IPO experience.*
- *Have a leading position in a growing market segment and are seeking to aggressively grow through acquisitions,*

> *post-IPO, with the goal being to dominate the office-based physician targeted media market.*

Set Clear Expectations

The third area of content that you should include in the Board Search Description describes the current board and sets expectations for members. This will help the candidate see how he or she would fit within the board team. Below is the Peak-Performance example of the "board" section of the Board Search Description (Exhibit 1c). It includes an overview of the current board members, a review of the constitution as it relates to expectations for board members, and a section on compensation. This description serves as a useful tool to use during the interviewing and recruiting process. It clearly lays out what the expectations and requirements are for board members. Note: If you are starting a new board, state that in the first part of the board section.

Exhibit 1c. Board Search Description: "Board" Section Example

---

Peak-Performance, Inc.
Board Search Description
(Created July, 2004)

An Overview of Our Current Board

- *Established in 1991.*
- *Currently four members (CEO plus three independent members). The independent members have found our board to be a rewarding, engaging learning experience and helpful to their own careers. Current board members include:*
  - *The CEO of the company (CEO since the company was founded, fourteen years ago)*
  - *Former president of a large and successful competitive firm that was sold (ten years high-growth business expertise in the same industry)*

- *Retired senior pharmaceutical marketing executive (thirty years related customer experience and currently chair of a start-up company)*
- *Seasoned operations executive (eighteen years operations expertise in an unrelated but highly reputable business)*

Board Expectations Overview

- *The Board Constitution provides clear expectations for board members. An overview of those expectations is reflected herein.*
- *The CEO will keep all board members informed between meetings and will send an organized board report before meetings, with ample time to prepare.*
- *Typically the board will meet four times a year for half-day morning meetings.*
- *It is expected that board members will be available for occasional phone conferences and infrequent emergency meetings, as appropriate.*
- *Three-year renewable term with annual review process (covered in board constitution, a separate document).*
- *Board members:*
  - *Are responsible and committed to the business.*
  - *Attend all meetings (ample advance notice provided).*
  - *Are punctual and prepared for every meeting.*
  - *Demonstrate a proficient and solid understanding of the business, markets, and competitive landscape.*
  - *Are accessible in between meetings, as needed (voice conference, etc., approximately five hours per quarter).*
  - *Offer expert, objective, and honest advice. We want you to be straightforward and apolitical.*
  - *Express point of view firmly but not harshly.*
  - *Challenge the CEO with the goal to help the business and to support the long-term interests of the shareholders.*
  - *Do not micromanage—board members address strategy and policy issues and do not lead or manage the day-to-day business.*

- *Identify opportunities and risks and contribute to solving strategic problems.*
- *Bring fresh ideas and new points of view for the CEO and management team to consider.*
- *Do not become "stale" (energy and enthusiasm remain high).*
- *Show initiative by constantly looking for ways to improve the business.*
- *Work well with other board members by respecting their opinions, not dominating the meetings, and listening to and building upon suggestions.*
- *Help the CEO network (i.e., identify good investment bankers, etc.).*
- *Hold the CEO accountable and are focused on improving the company's results, in part by ensuring management is accountable to those results.*
- *Are familiar with and in complete agreement with all of the terms and provisions of the company's Code of Conduct and Ethics (included as an attachment).*
- *Help with succession/exit plans, as appropriate.*
- *Hold all discussions and information in complete confidence (also covered in the Code of Conduct and Ethics; see Appendix 3).*

Board Compensation

- *$2,000 per meeting attended (typically four per year).*
- *$7,500 yearly retainer.*
- *Meaningful phantom stock plan to share in long-term upside potential based upon performance over time with stock conversion options (if and when an IPO or exit occurs).*
- *All reasonable travel and meeting expenses.*

Selecting Candidates

When you get to the point that you have multiple candidates to consider, it may be helpful to use a simple checklist selection tool called the *board candidate competency checklist.* An example follows in Exhibit 2. The board candidate competency checklist helps you clearly see the tradeoffs in expertise among candidates. Using a simple three-tier rating system, you can see the strengths and weaknesses of each candidate and compare those strengths across candidates. For instance, in the example in Exhibit 2, candidate E has significant financial expertise, plus she is the only financial expert with strong industry knowledge and prior board experience. She also has no negatives in areas that are important, such as integrity, working well with others, business judgment, and business passion. Thus, if Peak-Performance, Inc. is looking to recruit a financial expert (per the Board Search Description example), candidate E would be the best choice.

Exhibit 2. Example of a Board Candidate Competency Checklist

Peak-Performance, Inc. Board Candidate Competency Checklist

Key Strength Evaluation Criteria	Candidate Ratings				
	A	B	C	D	E
❖ Knowledge of Industry		+		√	+
❖ Business Passion	√	√	√	√	√
❖ Marketing Expertise	√	+			
❖ Operations Expertise				+	√
❖ Sales Expertise		√	√		
❖ Financial Expertise	+	√	√	√	+
❖ Sarbanes-Oxley Experience	√				+
❖ H R Expertise	√		+	√	
❖ Leadership Experience		+	√		√
❖ Prior Board Experience	√				√
❖ Integrity/Confidentiality	+	√	√	+	√
❖ Strategic Thinking Expertise		√		√	√
❖ Business Judgment	√	√	+	√	+
❖ Ideas/Creativity/Inventing	√	+			
❖ Expresses Own POV		√		√	√
❖ Challenges Status Quo	√		√		
❖ Works Well With Others	√	√		√	√
❖ Communication Skills	√	√	√	√	√
❖ Networking Benefits		√	√	√	+
❖ Family Business Expertise			√	+	√
❖ High Growth Expertise		√		√	
❖ Union Labor Expertise			+		
❖ Technology Expertise				+	

Key: Significant Strength/Exceptional expertise; +
Some Competence/Some expertise; √
Not a Strength/No expertise; **blank** (no symbol)

Never Stop Scouting

Continuously scout for new board members. Even if you have a full board, do not stop searching. Keep a file of potential board members. You never know when you may lose a good board member, have to replace a bad one or add another expert as your business evolves. It is advantageous to already have a head start on prospective members if and when the time comes that you will need a new board member.

Retaining Board Members

Retaining board members is important. It takes significant time and expense to identify, recruit, and train board members. Similar to good employees, you want to retain high-performing board members. There are a number of suggestions to help with board member retention. They are covered within each of the 5 Steps and summarized below:

> ➤ **Properly Define Requirements**—This prevents having to let a board member go because the company did not do its homework in properly defining what expertise and other requirements it needed.
> ➤ **Check for Good Chemistry**—This is difficult to define but very important. Each board member must work well on the team. Using the "tummy test" can help ensure the right chemistry is present.
> ➤ **Set Clear Expectations**—No one likes to be jerked around. When expectations are clearly and properly defined, effective board members are more likely to stay with the company.
> ➤ **Use Time Efficiently**—No one likes to waste time; especially competent board members. When you demonstrate that board meetings are well-run, it minimizes board member frustration.
> ➤ **Use Time Wisely**—Everyone likes to be on a winning team. If the board is working on the right things, the company will more likely be winning.
> ➤ **Compensate Fairly**—Most board members do not participate primarily for the money. However, everyone likes

to be valued. Paying board members fairly demonstrates that board members are valued.

> **Protect From Unforeseen Risks**—This has become very important, given the high media attention on corporate fraud, scandals, and failures. In fact, it may be difficult, if not impossible, to find good board candidates for a publicly traded company without adequate insurance. Board members should not be placed in a vulnerable or unnecessary high-risk position.

> **Build Relationships**—This is just as effective as it is with customers and employees. People like to feel connected to other people.

> **Listen and Act**—A great way to retain good board members is to demonstrate that you hear their suggestions. The best way to demonstrate that you are listening is to act on their good suggestions.

> **Recognize Good Performance**—Genuine recognition is one of the most effective ways to retain quality people on a team. Board members are no different. Besides, there are virtually no out-of-pocket costs associated with genuine recognition.

(Step 2)
THE RIGHT BOARD FRAMEWORK

2. Right Framework

1. Right Team

This section covers Step 2, The Right Framework. It begins with a discussion of what type of board(s) you should set up for your company. Next, you will find an easy-to-understand example of a board constitution and related code of conduct and ethics. Chapters covering board compensation, insurance, term limits, and retirement round out Step 2.

9. Establish the Right Board for Your Business Needs

"No stream can rise higher than its source."

— Frank Lloyd Wright, an original American architect and one of the world's greatest

9. Establish the Right Board for Your Business Needs

Two Different Types of Boards: Statutory and Advisory

The first part of Step 2 (Right Framework) is to ensure you have the right kind of board for your business needs. Should you establish a statutory (legal) board, an advisory board, or both? These two types of boards are *very different* from a legal perspective. Based on the Board Governance Survey conducted by the author, the following table indicates how U.S. small to midsize businesses stack up with respect to their board profiles:

U.S. Small to Midsize Business Board Profile	
% With a Advisory or Statutory Board	71.4%
% Without an Advisory or Statutory Board	28.6%
% With Advisory Board	32.1%
% With Statutory Board	53.6%
% With Advisory *and* Statutory Boards	14.3%
Based on a Board Governance Survey that was conducted by the author in August 2004 among a broad range of U.S. businesses that had at least 50 employees and sales that ranged from $5 million on the low side to over $1 billion on the high side. N = 112.	

An advisory board has no legal obligations or powers. It typically serves at the pleasure of the CEO. In contrast, a legal or "statutory" board is appointed by the shareholders. It has definite restrictions and practices that it must follow to comply with the law. A statutory board is more complex, time consuming, and potentially more threatening to the leadership of a business than an advisory board. The state statutes and the articles of incorporation govern it. State laws vary. Due to the importance of setting up a corporation correctly (legally and financially) and the variability in laws, you should check with your legal and financial advisors for specifics on how to best establish board governance requirements.

A Statutory Board May Be Required

All corporations (other than an LLC) are required to have a board of directors. Thus, if your business is a C or Subchapter S corporation, by law, you will need a statutory board. While many small to midsize private businesses do not properly empower their statutory boards, technically the statutory board provides approval to the corporate bylaws and amendments to the articles of incorporation. The statutory board handles stock matters and establishes the dividend policies and most other major corporate transactions. The statutory board also provides a general legal and fiduciary oversight of the company for the benefit of the shareholders. Ultimate authority for management of the company is vested in the statutory board. Officers of the corporation are elected by and technically serve at the pleasure of the statutory board.

If you are involved with a public company, state and federal laws dictate the legal and fiduciary requirements and responsibilities of the board of directors. In addition, there are specific requirements from the stock exchanges to consider.

If you are currently involved in a closely held (i.e., private) business but someday anticipate an Initial Public Offering (IPO), you may want to set up a statutory board that can easily migrate to the requirements of a public company board. This will serve as a good training ground for establishing the disciplines such as an independent audit committee, proper audits, underpromising and overdelivering on results, for instance, that you will want to achieve when you go public.

Lastly, a company undergoing an IPO will have to comply with Sarbanes-Oxley, a law enacted in 2002 as a result of fraud and other abuses by Enron and other large, publicly traded companies. Sarbanes-Oxley will be covered in Chapter 23.

Why Consider an Advisory Board?

If your business is an LLC, you may want to consider an advisory board. It can provide many of the benefits of a statutory board without the hassles.

Beyond an LLC, there are other situations where an advisory board may be appropriate. An advisory board is voluntary. It is not required by law. As such, it does not have any of the regulatory and fiduciary requirements of a statutory board. Additionally, there are fewer liability concerns for its members. These could be meaningful enough reasons to set up a separate advisory board.

What's more, if losing control is a concern of the leaders, an advisory board may be the way to go. For example, some states allow for the creation of a close corporation agreement (subject to shareholder approval), which can be set up to reduce the requirements and power of a statutory board. If this is done, you can create and use an advisory board to focus on long-term strategic and policy advice.

Another important reason to consider an advisory board is that you may be able to attract better members with the reduction in fiduciary responsibilities, liabilities, and risk.

Lastly, an advisory board offers more flexibility as to what the board's purpose is and what it focuses on.

Summary of Requirements

Corporate governance is prescribed under state law and to some extent under federal law (Sarbanes-Oxley). Since state laws vary, there is not an absolute list of responsibilities. However, there are typical responsibilities that are required of a statutory board. These are shown below in Exhibit 3. As you can see, there are many responsibilities (including protecting company assets, management oversight and evaluation, monitoring of the company's performance, and review of company objectives and policies). An advisory board requires none of these duties. If you only have an advisory board (and do not have statutory board), you may want your advisory board to assume some of these responsibilities such as reviewing corporate objectives and evaluating management performance.

However, if you have both types of boards, the required duties should remain with the statutory board. As mentioned, states have different requirements. This is an area that is important to understand. Thus, ask your legal advisors what is best for your company.

Recommendation?

Each business situation is unique. It is too difficult to generalize. Therefore, it is not appropriate to make a recommendation as to what you should do for your specific business. However, if you do not have to have a statutory board, an advisory board may be preferred. It has significantly less risk for members. An advisory board will enable you to attract better candidates with less cost. An advisory board will also offer more flexibility.

If you must have a statutory board and decide to have an advisory board too, you should have separate members on each board (other than the inside members such as the CEO). In addition, you should obtain a resolution from the statutory board that approves the advisory board as an autonomous and separate entity that does not have the fiduciary and legal oversight powers of the statutory board.

Regardless of what type of board or boards you choose, it is a good idea to have your attorney(s) periodically review your board practices and minutes. This will keep them in the loop and it can help minimize potential issues that otherwise could occur if they were not informed.

Exhibit 3. Statutory vs. Advisory Board Requirements

Action or Duty	Statutory Board	Advisory Board
Adopt bylaws	Required	Not Required
Change bylaws	Required	Not Required
Approve amendments to articles	Required	Not Required
Sale of company	Required	Not Required
Sale of any significant assets	Required	Not Required
Merge company	Required	Not Required
Consolidate company	Required	Not Required
Dissolve company	Required	Not Required
Protect creditors (if dissolved)	Required	Not Required
Acquisition of another company	Required	Not Required
Issue stock	Required	Not Required
Declare dividends	Required	Not Required
Repurchase stock	Required	Not Required
Review/approve corp. objectives	Required	Not Required
Monitor performance	Required	Not Required
Elect company officers	Required	Not Required
Select competent management	Required	Not Required
Establish officer compensation	Required	Not Required
Evaluate management performance	Required	Not Required
Protect shareholder interests	Required	Not Required
Ensure ethical behavior	Required	Not Required

10. How to Develop a Useful Board Constitution

"Common sense often makes good law."

— William O. Douglas, a United States Supreme Court Justice who served for nearly thirty-seven years (longer than any other)

10. How to Develop a Useful Board Constitution

Many small to midsize companies do not have clear written expectations for their directors. Specifically, over 77 percent claimed that they did not have a written role description for their boards (based on the Board Governance Survey conducted by the author).

This chapter shows you how to create a simple yet effective written board constitution, one that you can use to establish responsibilities and to set the right expectations for board members. It will go into detail and describe how to draft a useful board constitution. This is an essential part of Step 2 *(Right Framework)*. Unlike the articles of incorporation or an operating agreement, the board constitution is not intended to be a legal document on board governance. Rather, its purpose is *to set specific and clear expectations and responsibilities for members of a company board of directors or an advisory board.*

In a private company, the articles of incorporation (including the corporate bylaws) or the operating agreement (in the case of an LLC) cover the legal requirements for corporate governance. Since these documents can vary greatly by business and state, and there are a lot of legal nuances, we will not discuss them specifically in this book. However, these important legal documents should be discussed with and prepared by competent legal counsel and reviewed by the company's accountants.

A Board Constitution Sets Clear Expectations. It Is Different from the Articles of Incorporation

The easiest way to think of a board constitution is to view it as a written set of guidelines so that advisory or statuary board members know what to expect, and in part, how to perform. Examples and suggestions will be provided to help you create a board constitution that is useful to your specific needs.

All companies have bylaws, or if an LLC, an operating agreement which contain specific legal and fiduciary language. The board constitution is a different document. It is not a legal concept or legal requirement.

You do not want to overload the constitution with confusing legal details. The board constitution should be straightforward—you want to ensure that there is clear *alignment of expectations* among the members of the board. The KISS principle (Keep It Simple, Stupid) was a favorite of Ray Kroc, the founder of McDonald's. It has served that company well over the years. This principle is useful to apply when writing your board constitution.

So, what requirements and expectations do you include in the constitution? There is an example of a board constitution provided in Appendix 2. Portions of that example are also included and discussed below. The board constitution is not very complex. It contains three sections: 1) Statement of Purpose; 2) board member role description; and 3) board parameters. Each of these sections of the board constitution will be explained using specific examples in the pages that follow.

Clear Purpose

The board constitution should clearly explain why you have a board. This will also help frame your requirements and expectations for board members. As shown in Exhibit 4a (the constitution's Statement of Purpose), there is little ambiguity as to why the board exists.

Exhibit 4a. Example of the Board Constitution "Statement of Purpose" Section

---

Peak-Performance, Inc.
Board Constitution
(Created May 1993, last amended August 2004)

Statement of Purpose

❖ *To maximize long-term profitability and shareholder value.*

❖ *To help Peak-Performance, Inc. achieve its mission and long-term goals.*

❖ *To provide an invaluable source of outside, informed and independent stimulation and advice that helps the company reach its next level of success.*

❖ *To ensure a disciplined strategic planning approach is deployed that encompasses client needs, the company's competitive situation, market position, external trends and financial performance.*

❖ *To help the CEO make key decisions that affect the overall strategic direction of the company.*

❖ *To hold the CEO accountable to the plan and related results.*

❖ *To ensure appropriate company policies are in place and enforced.*

❖ *To serve as a court of appeals to senior management.*

❖ *To ensure a prudent and effective succession plan is in place.*

❖ *To assist the company in opening doors for opportunities (help network).*

Align Requirements and Expectations

It is also a good idea to define a board member's role to ensure alignment of requirements and expectations. The board member role description shown below provides an example of how to do this. The written requirements and expectations should improve alignment.

Of course, you should adapt the role description to your specific business and board needs.

Exhibit 4b. Example of the Board Constitution "Role Description" Section

---

Peak-Performance, Inc.
Board Constitution

<u>Board Member Role Description — Every Member:</u>

❖ *Is responsible and committed to the business.*

❖ *Attends all meetings and is punctual and prepared for every meeting.*

❖ *Demonstrates a proficient and solid understanding of the business, markets, and competitive landscape.*

❖ *Is accessible in between meetings, as needed (voice conference, etc., approximately five hours per quarter).*

❖ *Offers expert, objective, and honest advice.*

❖ *Is straightforward and apolitical. Expresses own point of view firmly but not harshly. Challenges the CEO with the goal to help the business and to support the long-term interests of the shareholders.*

❖ *Does not micromanage — addresses strategy and policy issues and does not lead or manage the day-to-day business.*

❖ *Helps the company invent. Brings fresh ideas and new points of view for the CEO and management team to consider.*

❖ *Does not become "stale" (energy and enthusiasm remain high).*

❖ *Shows initiative by constantly looking for ways to improve the business.*

❖ *Works well with other board members and management, in part by respecting their opinions and not dominating board meetings. Further, demonstrates a willingness to work with other members by listening to and building upon suggestions.*

❖ *Identifies opportunities and risks and contributes to solving strategic problems.*

- ❖ *Helps the CEO network.*
- ❖ *Holds the CEO accountable and is focused on improving the company's results, in part by ensuring management is accountable to those results.*
- ❖ *Participates in and is receptive to an annual evaluation (see Board Evaluation Form in Appendix 6).*
- ❖ *Conducts an annual review of the CEO's performance (see CEO Evaluation Form in Appendix 8).*
- ❖ *Is familiar with and in complete agreement with all of the terms and provisions of the Company's Code of Conduct and Ethics (included as an attachment).*
- ❖ *Helps with succession/exit plans, as appropriate.*
- ❖ *Holds all discussions and information in complete confidence (also covered in the Code of Conduct and Ethics; see Appendix 3).*

Board Parameters

The board constitution should set forth understandable parameters or "boundaries of operation." They can cover a range of areas from the number of members, to board terms, and retirement. As shown below in Exhibit 4c, simple guidelines are clearly set forth for the board of Peak-Performance, Inc. Of note, much of the procedural activity required for a statutory board is not necessary for an advisory board. Thus, for an advisory board, you should omit items such as the voting-related parameters. Items that may not be appropriate for an advisory board are denoted with an asterisk in the example below.

Exhibit 4c. Example of the Board Constitution "Board Parameters" Section

---

Peak-Performance, Inc.
Board Constitution

<u>Board Parameters</u>

❖ **Independent Members**—*The board will have independent experts who have no inside or direct affiliation or conflicts with the company (excludes employees, family members, suppliers, and the like). A majority of members will be independent.*

❖ **Number of Members** — *The board will contain no less than three and no more than six members. There will be no more than two inside members (CEO and one other, if needed). A majority of independent members will be maintained at all times.*

❖ ***New Members** — *New board members will require the majority approval of the shareholders (assumes Peak Performance, Inc. remains a closely held business).*

❖ **Chair**—*The CEO will act as the board Chair. The Chair will preside over meetings and be responsible for establishing the agenda with input from the board.*

❖ **Secretary** — *The Chair will designate a Secretary whose responsibility will be to record all of the board minutes.*

❖ **Meetings** — *The board will meet four to five times a year for half-day morning meetings.*

❖ **Attendance** — *It is expected that all board members will attend all meetings (unless there is a true emergency). Board members are to be punctual and come prepared for every meeting. Board members are also expected to be available for occasional phone conferences and infrequent emergency meetings, as appropriate.*

❖ **Communication** — *The Chair is responsible for sending an organized board report before meetings and for keeping all board members informed between meetings.*

❖ ****Voting Protocol***—*The board will use an established voting process. Specifically, board topics, actions or resolutions requiring a vote will start with an open discussion. After the open discussion, the Chair will call for a motion. If a motion is made, the Chair will then ask for a second to the motion. Objections will be considered and discussed. A verbal count of all those in favor and all those opposing the motion will be summarized. The vote will be concluded with a declaration that the motion has been accepted or rejected, contingent upon the vote.*

❖ ****Majority Rules*** *— A majority of member's votes will rule.*

❖ ****Split Votes*** *— If there is a tie, the Chair will cast the deciding vote.*

❖ ****Recorded*** *— Anything that is voted on will be recorded by the Secretary and reflected in the minutes.*

❖ ***Code of Conduct and Ethics***—*Each board member will be familiar with and in agreement with all of the terms and provisions of the Company's Code of Conduct and Ethics ("Code," see attached). Annually, each board member will be asked to certify that he or she is in compliance with the Code.*

❖ ***Board Terms*** *— Board terms will be for three years. Contingent upon satisfactory performance, they are renewable indefinitely up until retirement age is reached.*

❖ ***Retirement*** *— There is mandatory retirement at age seventy-five.*

❖ ***Board Evaluations*** *— Every board member will undergo an annual performance review process (see the Board Evaluation Form in Appendix 6). If performance is below an average of a "5" rating, the board member will be asked to resign.*

❖ ****Committees*** *— There will be no committees.*

*Not recommended for an advisory board

Quality, Not Quantity

Many state statutes require minimum board sizes for statutory boards. For example, in Ohio, if there are three or more shareholders, there must be at least three board members. For an advisory board, there are no size restrictions.

The board constitution should establish board size. For a statuary board, it should comply with state law requirements. The guiding principle for the number of members should be to obtain enough experts to effectively achieve the company's goals. For a small to midsized, company, three to six *outside* independent members (experts) should be adequate. Any fewer than three, you lose diversity and breadth of expertise. Any more than six board members, you have members who are not heard. They can become lost in the dialogue of a typical meeting. Another argument against large boards is that it is more time-consuming to obtain input and harder to gain commitment than with a smaller board. There tends to be a diminishing return on effort after about six outside board members.

Majority of Independent Members

Unfortunately, the Board Governance Survey conducted by the author showed that only 30 percent of small to midsize companies had a majority of independent board members.

Small to midsized, private businesses should have very few *inside* members. This may be one of the toughest issues a private company CEO faces when establishing a board. There are various constituents (family members, consultants, investors, senior managers, and minority shareholders) who may lobby for a position on the board. At a *minimum,* you should establish an even ratio of outside (independent) to inside members. Ideally, you should have a board with a majority of independent members. If you want to be true to an independent board's purpose (other than a family business that is transferring ownership to the next generation or an entrepreneurial business that has venture investments), the only justifiable candidates for an inside board position are the CEO, CFO or COO. Otherwise, board meetings will have a tendency turn into executive team meetings. The board can lose its objectivity, long-term strategic focus, and infusion of outside expertise. Ultimately, its overall effectiveness will dwindle. However, insiders should be invited to select meetings (or parts of select meetings), as appropriate.

Clear Voting and Decision Process

For a statutory board, the bylaws should stipulate the voting process. For an advisory board, a voting process is unnecessary and not recommended. Further, from a liability standpoint, if an advisory board votes like a statutory board, it could be deemed to be acting like a statutory board. Therefore, it could be exposed from a liability perspective.

For statutory boards, the board constitution is a good place to explain the voting protocol. Does a majority rule? This should be clearly answered in the board constitution. Another point to be crystal clear on is who has the final say if there is a split vote. An example of how to address this is shown in the board parameters section of the constitution as shown in Exhibit 4c and in Appendix 2.

Code of Conduct and Ethics

A code of conduct and ethics is different than the corporate bylaws. It is also different than the board constitution but is intricately linked to it. It is a pragmatic document. The code of conduct and ethics ("Code") goes beyond a statement of rules. It details fundamental company principles. These principles help board members to understand corporate policies and how they should be enforced. There are a few guidelines that help determine if your company has a good Code. First, a good Code should preclude anything that is illegal. There should be no inconsistencies between a company's laws and civil law. Second, a good Code should have an element of fairness—of balance for all stakeholders. Lastly, it should pass the "tummy test" and encourage board members to do the right thing in all situations.

It is good business practice to articulate a Code for a small to midsize private business. This will help board members understand how to deal with important issues such as fairness, integrity, conflicts of interest, and the like. Net, the Code helps board members to better understand the requirements and expectations of the company.

Specific items that should be considered in the Code include:

> Integrity (honesty)
> A Conflict of Interest Statement
> Compliance with Regulations
> Proper Use of Company Assets
> Confidentiality
> Fair Dealing
> Reporting Illegal or Unethical Behavior

The Code is not a complete or perfect set of standards. Having too many requirements can reduce employee, officer, and board member understanding of the Code. This, in turn, will reduce effectiveness. Thus, it is a good idea to limit the number of items in a Code to fewer than ten, and ideally five to seven.

A good Code translates the company's ideals into specific behaviors. A properly crafted and executed Code can reinforce the company's culture. Examples should be given of noncompliance so that it is clear to the reader what the ground rules are. The Code should be created with board and executive team involvement. It should not be a boilerplate list. Rather, it should be unique to the company, just as a company's culture should be unique.

In addition to creating the document, to be effective, the Code must be consistently communicated to employees, officers, and board members. Even more important, if a violation occurs, the Code must be enforced. Appendix 3 shows a complete example of Peak-Performance's Code.

The section on conflicts of interest is included below in Exhibit 5. As you can see, there are good examples of what constitutes a violation of Peak-Performance's conflict of interest policy. A caveat is also stated that the examples do not cover every situation.

Exhibit 5. Example of a Conflict of Interest Statement

Peak-Performance, Inc.
CODE OF CONDUCT AND ETHICS

Conflicts of Interest — *A "conflict of interest" occurs when an individual's private interest interferes or appears to interfere in any way with the interests of the Company as a whole. A conflict of interest can arise when an employee, officer, or director takes actions or has interests that may make it difficult to perform his or her Company work objectively and effectively.*

For example, a conflict of interest would arise if an employee, officer, or director (or a member of his or her family), receives improper personal benefits as a result of his or her position in the Company. Any material transaction or relationship that could reasonably be expected to give rise to a conflict of interest should be discussed with the Code of Ethics Contact Person.

This Code does not attempt to describe all possible conflicts of interest that could develop. Potential or real conflict of interest situations should always be discussed with the Code of Ethics contact person. Anything that would present a conflict for an employee, officer, or director would likely also present a conflict if it involved a family member. Clear conflict of interest situations involving employees, officers, and directors in supervisory positions or who have discretionary authority may include but are not limited to the following:

- *Any significant ownership interest in any supplier, competitor, or customer;*
- *Any outside business activity that detracts from an individual's ability to devote appropriate time and attention to their responsibilities with the Company;*
- *Any consulting or employment relationship with any supplier or competitor;*
- *Being in the position of supervising, reviewing, or having any influence on the job evaluation, pay, or benefit of any immediate family member;*

- *The receipt of non-nominal gifts or excessive entertainment from any person or company with which the Company has current or prospective business dealings; and*
- *Selling anything to the Company or buying anything from the Company, except on the same terms and conditions as comparable employees, officers, or directors are permitted to purchase or sell.*

A good example of how to cover reporting violations is shown below in Exhibit 6. A few points that make this section meaningful include the notion of an open-door policy, and the inclusion of a "whistleblower provision" that prohibits the company from taking action against informants. This also helps comply with the private company "whistleblower" requirement of Sarbanes-Oxley (covered in Chapter 23).

Exhibit 6. Example of Reporting Violations Statement

Peak-Performance, Inc.
CODE OF CONDUCT AND ETHICS

Reporting Violations—*The Company encourages employees, officers, and directors to report violations and make appropriate suggestions regarding the business practices of the Company. Specifically, any employee, officer, or director who becomes aware of any existing or potential violation of this Code is required to notify the Code of Ethics contact person promptly. Failure to do so is a violation of this Code.*

Employees, officers, and directors are expected to report promptly to The Code of Ethics contact person, suspected violations of law, and the Company's policies (including this Code) so that the Company can take corrective action. No action may be taken or threatened against an employee, officer, or director for reporting violations, or making suggestions in conformity with the procedures described above, unless, the employee, officer, or director acts with willful disregard of the truth.

Another important item to include in the Code is clarity as to who violations should be brought to for resolution. The Peak-Performance example does this in the beginning of the Code document as follows:

All employees, officers, and directors of the Company are expected to be familiar with the Code and to adhere to those principles and the procedures set forth in the Code that apply to them. For purposes of this Code, the "Code of Ethics contact person" will be:

- *For each member of the Board of Directors: the Chair, Chief Executive Officer, or the Chief Financial Officer.*
- *For Director-level or higher employees (e.g., Vice President of Operations, Director of Product Development, etc.): the Chief Executive Officer.*
- *For all other employees: the Director of the department in which they are employed.*

Committee Governance

The board constitution should establish committees, if needed (not recommended for an advisory board). Smaller, private businesses generally do *not need committees.* However, there may be exceptions. If unique and specific expertise or focus may be required, consider a separate committee, possibly on a temporary basis. For public company boards, committees to consider (some are required, such as the audit committee) include:

❖ **Audit Committee**—independently monitors and evaluates the financial and audit processes of the business.
❖ **Compensation Committee**—independently determines the appropriate compensation for management and the board. Recommends compensation using appropriate and objective benchmark data.
❖ **Executive Committee** — a subset of the board authorized to act on behalf of the board when it is urgent or all members of the board are unable to get together to discuss a matter.

- ❖ **Nominating and Governance Committee**—independently nominates officers and board members.
- ❖ **Succession Committee**—independently helps select the next CEO (oftentimes part of the Nominating and Governance Committee).

Committees Should Be Independent

If you have a genuine need for a committee, it should have independence. For example, the compensation committee should have complete authority to hire the appropriate outside experts it needs to determine the right officer compensation. Likewise, the audit committee should *independently* choose the accounting and auditing firm, subject to the entire board's approval (this is required by Sarbanes-Oxley for publicly traded companies).

Committees should have their own charter and defined roles (describing the expertise or competencies of the members). These should be communicated and understood by all board members and management. Of note, if Sarbanes-Oxley is relevant to your business, Chapter 23 has a more detailed discussion on the audit committee as it pertains to Sarbanes-Oxley requirements and compliance.

What About an Executive Committee?

Executive committees are generally *unnecessary* for small to medium-size businesses. In fact, having an executive committee can actually weaken the quality of the board members and, subsequently, board effectiveness. Why would you want to be on a board if you are not on the executive committee? What competent person would want to be a "second-class board member?" However, some companies have executive committees whose purpose was described previously and may be considered when the company has a large number of board members. As a reminder, executive committees are not required or recommended for an advisory board.

11. Tips on Board Compensation

"Dollars not only count, they rule."

—Charles Thomas Walker, a former slave who became an early proponent of civil rights

11. Tips on Board Compensation

Most Board Members Don't Serve for the Money, But...

A sometimes overlooked part of the right framework (Step 2) is a good board compensation plan. Even though money is typically not the main reason for serving on a board, you should pay fairly. Make it worth the board member's effort, both in terms of listening to and acting upon their good advice and in terms of paying them a fair financial remuneration.

As with many things in life, you typically get what you pay for. Everyone has choices of how they invest their time; especially talented board candidates. You do not want to short-change them on compensation. Why create an incentive to use their precious time elsewhere? You want the board members to feel valued and respected.

Small to midsize companies that pay more to board members claim their boards help them maximize profits better than those that pay less. For example, companies that pay well rated their boards an average of 8.4 on the boards' performance in maximizing profit (based on a 10-point scale where "10" represents highly effective and "1" represents not effective). This compares favorably to companies that pay their board members on the low side of the pay scale. Specifically, as shown in the chart below, they rated their boards an average of 5.5 on the boards' performance in maximizing profit.

Annual Board Member Pay	Maximizing Profit Rating
> $15,000 Per Board Member	8.4
< $5,000 Per Board Member	5.5
Based on a Board Governance Survey conducted in August 2004 using a ten- point scale where 10 = "highly effective" and 1 = "not effective." *n* = 112	

Avoid Board Members Who Serve for the Money

While you do want to pay your board members well, you *do not want anyone on your board who is doing it primarily for the money* or the money represents a material portion of their income. It is much better to recruit board members who have a passion to share their expertise. Money should be a secondary consideration.

You should look at board compensation as a means for rewarding the behaviors you want to instill in your board members.

There are three general types of board compensation to consider. Two are short-term compensation, the meeting fee and the retainer. The third is a longer-term compensation arrangement (stock incentives, phantom stock, and the like). You can offer one or any combination of fees.

Meeting Fees

Most companies typically pay a meeting fee. Meeting fees are paid for board meeting preparation, attendance, and participation. There is a wide range of consideration. The meeting fee can vary anywhere from a couple of hundred dollars up to $10,000 per meeting attended.

In general, meeting fees for small to midsize private companies average in the $1,000 to $3,000 range (at the time of this publication). If the board has committees, the committee members are often remunerated at a higher level than non-committee members (typically at a 50 percent premium per meeting).

Meeting fees in small to midsize businesses are generally only paid to the independent board members. Officers, the CEO, or other inside members should already be adequately compensated and should not be paid board or committee fees.

Pay for Attendance

If an independent board member is unable to attend a board meeting, he or she should not be paid a meeting fee for the missed meeting.

Here is a simple tip to reinforce the behavior of participating in the board meeting. Have the checks drawn up before the meeting. Hand them out at the end of each meeting. This will tangibly reward the positive behavior of attending and partaking in the meeting.

Retainer Fees

Many small to midsize companies pay a retainer fee in addition to a meeting fee. As with a meeting fee, the retainer fee is typically only paid to the independent board members (not the inside board members).

The retainer fee is paid for overall participation on the board. It should also compensate for board duties and time spent between meetings. If you plan to have a lot of between-meeting board work, you should have a higher retainer. If not, then a lower retainer fee is appropriate. If you plan to only use the board during meetings, you may want to consider not paying a retainer fee. However, if you do not pay a retainer fee, the meeting fees should be on the higher side.

Regarding retainer fees, they can range from zero to more than $25,000 per year. Typically, $5,000 to $15,000 is the approximate average yearly retainer fee for small to midsize companies in the U.S. (at the time of this publication). The retainer fee should be adjusted higher or lower contingent upon the quality of board member expertise you desire. Other factors to consider include the size and stage of your company, how much you pay in other remuneration (meeting fees and long-term incentives), and how much you want to reward your board members. You can check with your accounting firm to get a better sense of what the local market is paying board members with the experience and expertise you desire.

Long-Term Incentives

Long-term incentives, such as shares of stock, stock options, Stock Appreciation Rights (SARs), phantom stock arrangements, and the like can be motivating to board members. Any long-term incentive plan should be worked out with your legal and financial advisors to ensure they are implemented properly, and you and your board members understand the legal and tax consequences of your arrangements.

While more complicated than meeting or retainer fees, it may make sense to offer long-term compensation arrangements for board members. The reason is simple. These incentive programs align board behaviors with long-term company goals. As mentioned before, *you get what you pay for.* The highest leverage value of a board is to help you with strategy and policy issues. By definition, strategy and policy issues should lead to long-term results. Why not reward the board according to those results?

Pay for Performance

There are several long-term incentive alternatives you may want to consider, including paying board members in stock (or options) based upon their *performance.* Performance-based stock grants or options can help align board member behavior with the long-term health of the company. The more value the stock and/or options have, the more likely the board will pay attention to the company's long-term well-being. The one caution is that a private company will need to develop a path to liquidity other than through the sale of the company. Otherwise, the board could be motivated to sell the company for the wrong reasons. You want to align expectations with the behaviors you desire. Anything that presents a potential conflict of allegiance should be avoided.

Deferred compensation plans, such as phantom stock or 401(k) plans, are other options to consider. A potential caution for broadly traded public companies is the sale of long-term incentives, such as stock. Sarbanes-Oxley and the SEC have specific rules and requirements. These rules should be clearly understood by all board members and management. Any long-term board compensation plans should be reviewed with your lawyers and accountants to ensure proper compliance with laws and regulations.

If you are going to pay with a combination of short-term (meeting and/or retainer fees) and long-term compensation (stock, options, phantom stock, and the like), a good principle to consider is a 50/50 balance between short- and long-term compensation. Of note, you should value the long-term compensation in today's dollars, not a projection of a future appreciated value. That will enable a board member to realize an appreciation in value, should the company perform well. To be clear, the 50/50 principle is in no way a hard and fast rule. You can adjust the balance between short- and long-term compensation as you see fit.

Higher Statutory Board Fees

In general, compensation for a statutory board should be higher than for an advisory board. The reason is simple. There are greater risks associated with being a member of a statutory board.

Insurance

Insurance is an important expense item that continues to escalate in cost. From a recruiting viewpoint, having appropriate insurance can make a big difference in your ability to attract high-quality board members. D&O insurance is a complicated area and should be pursued using a good insurance agent. The next chapter (Chapter 12, *Ways to Protect Board Members*) goes into more detail on this important topic.

Promptly Pay Expenses

As noted in the Board Search Description (Appendix 1), it is appropriate to pay reasonable travel expenses. A fair approach is to pay board member expenses the same way the company pays executive employee travel expenses.

Another good practice is to ask board members to submit their expenses for reimbursement after each meeting, similar to the process an employee goes through in submitting expenses for reimbursement after they travel.

Here's a tip to make it easier on your board members to promptly receive their travel expenses. Include an expense report with each board package. If it is easier for board members to use their own expense forms, that should be OK, as long as their expense report properly and accurately captures the board member travel expenses. The point is, make the process easy on the board members and pay the expenses promptly.

Board Budget Considerations

A good business board will have an expense associated with it. However, the returns on a nominal investment are typically outstanding. Tenfold and higher returns are feasible and commonly achieved. The total yearly expense that you can plan on for an advisory board or board of director's budget will vary. The budget will depend on several key variables, including:

- How many independent members there are
- The number of meetings per year
- Compensation in the form of meeting fees (if any)
- Compensation in the form of a yearly retainer (if any)
- Compensation in the form of long-term incentives (if any)
- Travel expenses (if any)
- Entertainment/meeting expenses
- D&O insurance (if any)

Average yearly total fees per board member for small to midsize companies were approximately $12,000 (based on the Board Governance Survey). This total can vary greatly according to the quality of board member expertise desired, the size and risks of the company, and local market conditions. To put this into perspective, a Fortune 1000 board member was paid an average of $89,000 in 2002 according to Korn Ferry data. This average has increased dramatically in recent years with the advent of Sarbanes-Oxley.

Using a few assumptions, we can put together a typical budget for a small to midsize company board. We will assume a well- run company with sales in the $35 million range with no unusual risks. Further assumptions are four independent (outside) members, four meetings per year (at $2,000 per meeting) and a $7,500 yearly retainer. The meeting fees and yearly retainer fees are about the average for a small to midsize company board at time of publication. We will assume one member travels via airplane, the other three are local. Based on these assumptions, our typical budget looks like the following:

$32,000 Meeting Fees	(Four independent members @ $2,000 per member multiplied by four meetings)
$30,000 Retainer Fees	(Four independent members multiplied by $7,500 yearly retainer per member)
$4,800 Travel	(One independent member @ $1,200 per meeting multiplied by four meetings)
$1,000 Entertainment	(Four meetings multiplied by $250 per meeting for food, and other miscellaneous expenses)

$67,800 Total*

---

* Excludes D&O insurance. This can vary greatly according to business risks and other factors.

The budget for a small to midsize company board can vary widely from around $25,000 in total to over $160,000. On the low side, if you figure three independent members at four meetings, a $5,000 yearly retainer, no travel, the total yearly budget would be just north of $25,000. On the other hand, if you assume five independent members, five meetings a year, and a $15,000 yearly retainer fee per independent member, air travel for two members, the total will exceed $160,000 per year. The table on the next page details these budget ranges from low to high. Of note, midsize companies with more at stake should pay on the higher side. Smaller companies with limited risk may not have to pay as much.

Projected Total Yearly Board Budget Ranges			
Budget Item	Low	Medium	High
# Outside Members	3	4	5
# Meetings	4	4	5
Fee Per Meeting	$1,000	$2,000	$3,000
Total Meeting Fees	$12,000	$32,000	$75,000
Retainer Per Member	$5,000	$7,500	$15,000
Total Retainer Fees	$15,000	$30,000	$75,000
Travel	None	$4,800	$12,000
Entertainment	$400	$1,000	$1,500
Total Budget*	$27,400	$67,800	$163,500

* Note: The figures used in the above charts assume small to midsize companies and were reliable at the time of publication. You should check with your accountants and other local experts to verify what is relevant for your market. Also note that the above totals exclude any long-term board member compensation expense. If you have a long-term board compensation plan, it should be reviewed with your accountants. Contingent upon the plan you choose, there could be an annual expense associated with the long-term board member compensation plan. Finally, the figures do not include D&O insurance premiums. Annual D&O insurance can vary widely from a low of about $15,000 for a small, low-risk company with limited coverage to well over $500,000 for a midsize company with significant sales, assets, and risks.

12. Ways to Protect Board Members

"Human life, its growth, its hopes, fears, loves, et cetera, are the result of accidents."

—Bertrand Russell, a British philosopher, logician, and essayist

12. Ways to Protect Board Members

Why Consider Board Insurance?

The answer is simple. There are two main reasons. First, you want to protect your company, its officers and directors against catastrophic risks. Second, you will recruit better board members if you reduce their risk. Better board members should lead to better business results. Experienced board members may not even agree to join your board without proper insurance.

According to the Board Governance Survey conducted by the author, 27 percent of small to midsize companies with *statuary* boards did not have D&O insurance. Unfortunately, we live in a society that likes to litigate. Thus, it is a good idea to protect your board members if you are operating a statutory board, especially if it is a broadly traded public company or it is a closely held private company that is operating with higher-than-normal risks to board members.

Without insurance, you expose the company in the case where it has a clause in the bylaws that indemnifies officers and directors against personal liability for actions taken on behalf of the company or you expose the directors (and officers) to potentially large risks.

Even if the company has excellent business practices, it is a good idea to protect it from unforeseen risks. There are various areas that are worth protecting, such as negligence and fiduciary duties, employment practices, discrimination, and environmental issues. If you have an advisory board (and do not have a statuary board), you may still want to consider insurance. However, it is not as essential as it is for a private statuary board or for a publicly traded company board.

Consider D&O Insurance

The most common type of board insurance is called D&O insurance. D&O is short for "Directors and Officers." The purpose of a D&O insurance policy is to protect directors and officers of a company from liability in the event of a lawsuit against them claiming wrongdoing in connection with the company's business and its practices. It insures against errors and omissions of directors. Normally, it covers litigation expenses for board members. You should review your options with professional insurance agents who specialize in D&O insurance.

D&O Risks and Expenses Are Rising

Post-Sarbanes-Oxley, D&O insurance premiums have increased sharply, especially for public companies. The market may be better for private companies. However, recognize that the underwriting process is somewhat subjective for small to midsize private companies. It is difficult for D&O underwriters to accurately determine the chances that a specific private company will be sued. This is especially difficult for the myriad smaller private companies in the U.S. For perspective, based upon the U.S. Small Business Administration, Office of Advocacy, and using their calculations from the U.S. Census Bureau, Statistics of U.S. Businesses, they show that there are over 250,000 small business in the United State that have at least twenty-five but fewer than fifty employees. Imagine the task of an insurance company trying to determine potential liabilities among the different small companies that have different financials, business models, and compete in different industries, markets, and the like. Thus, it is important to provide information to the underwriter so that they have a realistic picture of the business and its associated risks.

Claims Can Come from Various Sources

Insurance claims are likely to come from the following areas:

➢ **Employees** (disgruntled employees, sexual harassment, discrimination, wrongful termination claims, and the like).

➤ **Shareholders** (shareholders upset about management decisions — includes minority shareholders, family members, charitable trusts, heirs, etc.). As a side note, an IPO-bound company will have many more shareholders after it goes public.

➤ **Competitors** (competitors make claims for defensive and offensive reasons).

➤ **Customers** (unhappy customers make claims due to contract violations, poor performance, and the like).

➤ **Suppliers** (suppliers sue for misrepresentations, lenders/investors make claims when they experience unexpected losses, etc.).

➤ **Government** (the government may pursue workplace, safety, and environmental claims).

➤ **Miscellaneous** (this includes intellectual property claims, among others).

Pick a Good Agent with D&O Expertise

Of note, the following is written as if the reader were the actual person selecting an insurance agent and buying D&O insurance. The task of selecting an agent and buying D&O insurance may be delegated to a competent person on the executive team, such as the CFO. If that is the case, have that person review this chapter and explore other information and resources, as appropriate.

One of the most important steps you can take to obtain the right D&O insurance is to pick a good agent (broker) who *specializes* in D&O insurance underwriting. You do not want an agent who is a generalist. Your agent should have meaningful experience with D&O insurance. He or she will be an important guide in the D&O insurance process. A good agent or broker should analyze your business, recommend what types of insurance you need, and in what amounts. He or she will then shop the market to obtain the best buy for your money. A good agent can also show you ways to minimize risks, thereby helping to lower D&O insurance premium costs. The agent should also assist in the claims process.

There are several things you can do to improve the odds that you pick a good D&O insurance specialist. First, you should aggressively network. Other business leaders are a good source of leads, as are trade groups, your local chamber of commerce, peer learning groups, and other professional organizations. Look in particular for an agent you can trust. It is also beneficial to find one who knows your industry.

Ask prospective agents for references. Call the references. You should select an agent or broker who works with strong, established D&O insurance underwriters that have good claims records. Insurance companies are rated by independent ratings agencies. You should look for companies rated A- or higher.

Also examine the agent's credentials. Designations such as Chartered Financial Consultant (ChFC), Certified Insurance Counselor (CIC), or Registered Employee Benefits Consultant (REBC) designate that the agent has completed a course of study in that field. Agents who belong to trade groups and industry associations are more likely to keep their skills honed and their industry information up to date. Once you have selected an agent, invest the necessary time to work with that agent to come up with the proper D&O insurance coverage and options.

After you have received the D&O insurance policy, ask your agent to explain it to you in detail. You should fully understand the policy. Do not let the relationship with your agent end there. Keep your agent informed about any claims you file, or any developments in your business that may require a change in your D&O insurance coverage.

Tips on Buying D&O Insurance

As you consider D&O insurance, recognize that it can be very expensive and there are a lot of subtle nuances with the policies. However, there are specific steps that you can take to help an insurance agent accurately position your company so that it is placed in an appropriate D&O insurance risk category. Make sure you choose an insurance company that is well-qualified in underwriting in the D&O area.

D&O providers (underwriters) evaluate small to midsize private companies in similar ways that investors look at a company to determine if they want to invest or not. Key factors that D&O underwriters look at include (among others):

- How long has the company been in business?
- How strong are the financials? Specifically, how healthy are the income statement, balance sheet, and statement of cash flows?
- How strong are key financials metrics and ratios (current ratio, debt to equity, and the like)?
- In what business segment does the company compete? How well is it positioned in the market?
- How strong is the company's business model?
- How diverse is the company's customer base? Is the revenue stream reliable, growing, and consistent?
- How strong and experienced is the executive team?
- How solid are the human resource procedures? A lot of private company claims emerge from disgruntled employees; having good HR procedures minimize risks.
- Who are the auditors, legal counsel, and other key suppliers? Are the statements audited by a reputable firm?
- How strong is the board? Is it truly independent?
- What is the claims history? Have there been any claims in the past?

If you solicit bids for D&O insurance, you should provide an accurate assessment of the company's risks to potential insurance underwriters. This will help ensure you have the right coverage and protection.

D&O policies should be reviewed by the board periodically to ensure that the right protection and coverage is in place based upon the size and risks of the business. Recognize that there is a trend towards more exclusions (especially for fraud) and higher deductibles as costs escalate.

Ensure your company's bylaws allow indemnification by D&O insurance and in lieu of D&O insurance to cover costs incurred to the full extent of the law.

Here is a tip. If you have an advisory board in addition to a statutory board, make sure your D&O insurance agent is familiar with the scope of the advisory board's authority. If an advisory board is deemed to be making decisions (as opposed to recommendations), it could be deemed to have a fiduciary responsibility to the shareholders, causing potential exposure to lawsuits.

If you obtain D&O insurance, you should have a policy with continuing coverage. If you have an ongoing relationship with an insurance agent and underwriter and have had D&O insurance for a number of years with the same carrier, you should try and avoid re-signing a "warrantee statement" that specifies "no one in the company has any knowledge of any acts or circumstances that may give rise to a claim." Re-signing this waiver should be resisted. This warrantee statement was likely signed when your D&O insurance was first put into effect. If you sign it years later, a gap in coverage could technically occur.

Questions to Ask

Buying D&O insurance can be difficult. Unlike the purchase of a tangible asset, you cannot see it. It is difficult to know if you have the right amount of coverage and if you have the right things covered. Use your agent to help you sort through the following questions. These questions are by no means comprehensive. However, they are a good starting point:

Coverage Amount—What is the right coverage for our company? There are three main factors that will help you determine what is the right level of coverage for your business. The first is the magnitude of your revenues and assets. Obviously, the greater the level of sales and assets, the more there is at stake to lose. Larger companies typically require higher coverage levels. Of course, the D&O policy expense will increase commensurately with the coverage level.

The second factor that will help you determine what is the right amount of coverage for your company is an assessment of the risks associated with the company. Related to this is the company's appetite for risk. It is important to accurately present these risks. Otherwise, a future claim could be in jeopardy if it is shown that a company purposely hid information during the application process.

The third factor to help determine coverage is the company's future plans. Is it a high-growth company? If so, then coverage may need to be adjusted upward for anticipated growth. Conversely, if the company anticipates slow growth or declining sales, the amount of coverage may need to be adjusted downward, as appropriate.

Cancellation Provisions—With escalating premium costs, there is a trend towards more and more cancellation provisions. Thus, it is prudent to understand under what situations the underwriter can cancel the D&O policy.

What Is/Is Not Covered—Ask the agent (or underwriter) to detail precisely what is covered and what is not covered. This exercise can help prevent unfortunate situations later on, should a claim occur. It is better to know exactly what you are buying up front. Several specific areas worth probing include the following:

- **What Legal Fees Are Covered?** — Does the underwriter agree to advance the cost of legal fees in the event of a claim, or only to reimburse the company for costs paid out of the company's own pocket? The former option may cost more. However, it provides the company better protection.

- **Are Inside and Outside Limits Covered?** — Does the policy cover defense costs inside or outside the limits? If it only covers defense costs inside the limit, a policy with a $5 million limit, obligates the insurer to pay no more than $5 million for any one claim, including legal fees. If the policy covers defense costs outside the limit, the same $5 million policy obligates your insurer to pay claims costs and legal fees separately, with separate limits for each. Obviously, the "inside" limits policy will cost less. However, make sure you consider the extra risk if you choose this option.

- **Is the Company Covered Too?** — Does the D&O insurance policy cover the company as well as its directors and officers? Plaintiffs' attorneys routinely sue both directors and officers personally, and the company for which they are employed or on the board. It may be a good idea to consider a D&O insurance policy that covers all of these parties.

- **Are Employment Practices Covered?** — Does the coverage combine D&O and employment practices liability insurance in one policy? If so, make sure you buy a high enough limit of coverage. That's because a large D&O claim can leave you without adequate coverage against an employment practices suit. This could further expose the company. One of the largest sources for claims in small to midsize private companies is from employees. Thus, it is a good idea to insure directors (and officers) against wrongdoing under federal and state employment practices laws. These include claims for wrongful termination, sexual harassment, and discrimination.

- **Foreign Law Coverage** — For companies that do business internationally, it may be important to have a policy that covers legal actions brought forth under foreign laws.

- **Does The Policy Maintain Coverage?** — Board members should be protected for some time period after they retire for acts that occurred while they were board members. It is recommended that the policy maintain coverage for a number of years after a board member retires or resigns.

- **What Waivers Will Be Required?** — It is important to understand the ramifications of agreeing to waivers from a coverage and liability standpoint.

- **What Else Should I Have Asked?** — It is always a good idea to ask your agent and/or the underwriter: "What else should I have asked that I didn't?" This open-ended question can elicit important questions and answers, particularly when purchasing something for the first time or that you have limited experience with.

Buyer Beware

D&O insurance is complicated and can be costly. Like most new experiences, "caveat emptor" applies with purchasing D&O insurance. You should work with good insurance agents and underwriters who are honorable and knowledgeable. You should also have someone on your team (perhaps your attorney) read the D&O insurance policy very carefully. The devil can be in the details. It is important that you know what you are really buying.

IPO Bound?

If you are IPO bound, in order to obtain D&O insurance, the underwriters will want to ensure that you are Sarbanes-Oxley compliant. Sarbanes-Oxley is discussed in Chapter 23. There are many stringent requirements to comply with Sarbanes-Oxley. For example, you will need greater financial and internal controls. The board will have to be truly independent. You will need an independent audit committee with a financial expert on that committee. Loans to executive officers will be prohibited. A code of conduct and ethics will need to be in place. These are just a few of the Sarbanes-Oxley requirements that will need to be implemented for an IPO.

The 5 Steps Will Help

Having an effective, independent board will help position your company with respect to D&O insurance. Many of the suggestions found in this book can help minimize D&O insurance expenses. Additionally, they can improve the odds that you obtain D&O insurance on terms that are reasonable. To the underwriters, anything concrete that you can show that indicates your company is a good bet (lower risk) should help.

13. Board Term Guidelines

"People do not retire, they are retired by others."

—Duke Ellington, one of the world's greatest composers and musicians

13. Board Term Guidelines

What About Board Term Limits?

Term limits and board retirement are the last two points that we will cover in Step 2 (Right Framework). There has been an ongoing debate on the issue of term limits. Some board experts recommend them. Others do not.

On the one hand, companies that impose term limits argue that replenishing a board helps ensure fresh perspectives are brought forth. They believe new blood prevents a board from getting stale.

While this is a reasonable point to consider, the author's preference is to have specific *renewable terms coupled with an annual evaluation process* instead of imposing definite board term limits. As long as the board member is performing well *and* you have effective board evaluation and improvement processes in place, it does not make sense to remove a good board member.

The basis for this argument is the same as for professional sports. Does it make sense to "trade" or retire a high-performing player from a professional sports team (taking salary issues aside) just because he or she has been around for a long time? If the results are there, the player (i.e., board member) should remain unless there is clearly a better athlete (board candidate) available. Related to this is the point that long-term directors accumulate increasing insight into the company, its opportunities and challenges. These insights should lead to higher board member contributions.

Establishing specific *renewable* terms forces the board and the board member to evaluate on a periodic basis how the relationship is working. It also enables the board or the board member to more readily make a change if a change is required or desired. Annual board member reviews coupled with the potential for a renewable term have a miraculous effect on board member performance. This

139

process flushes out whether a board member has remained fresh or become stale, and it enables the board to retain a highly effective board member for many terms (as long as performance remains high).

Board Term Ranges

One to five years is the range for most company board terms. Three years is recommended for most private companies. It enables a board candidate enough time to come up to speed and effectively leverage his or her knowledge and expertise to help the business. On the other hand, it is on the outer limit for a checkpoint to determine how the relationship is working. Having an annual board member performance review shortens the three-year window between terms. It enables both parties to part ways if the relationship is not working, or to continue the relationship if it is working well.

Hire Slow, Fire Fast

The saying: "Hire slow and fire fast" has just as much relevance for board members as it does for employees. If you have to dismiss an ineffective board member, it is best to do this promptly. Prompt action is appropriate, assuming the board member does not wish to improve and has had a chance to improve. However, if the board member genuinely wants to improve and it is a reasonable bet that they can, they should be given a chance.

Stagger Board Terms

Another consideration with respect to board terms is to try to stagger them, if feasible. Specifically, do not have every board member's term expire in the same year. This will help minimize dramatic changes in board makeup (and potentially effectiveness) that could occur if several peak-performing board members were to depart at the same time. It will also spread out the board member recruiting effort.

What About Retirement?

There is an age where it does make sense to retire a board member. What is the right age for mandatory retirement? Anywhere from seventy to seventy-five years of age seems reasonable to consider, as long as periodic board member performance reviews are conducted. While board members at age seventy or seventy-five may seem too old, having renewable terms and an annual board member evaluation process will help prevent members from hanging on because of inertia.

(Step 3)
THE RIGHT BOARD PROCESS

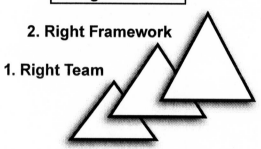

3. Right Process

2. Right Framework

1. Right Team

This section covers Step 3, The Right Process. It concentrates on effectively managing the board (operationally doing things right). It begins with tips on training board members. A comprehensive chapter on how to run effective board meetings concludes Step 3.

14. Training Board Members

"Teaching is not a lost art, but regard for it is a lost tradition."

—Jacques Barzun, an American writer, educator, historian, and former dean of Columbia University

14. Training Board Members

Train to Improve Effectiveness

Not many companies train their boards. According to the Board Governance Survey conducted by the author, less than 13 percent of companies had an organized board member training process in place. Training board members is an important part of the process of managing the board (Step 3). It is also important for board effectiveness. The more informed your board is on the company and its key opportunities and risks, the more likely there will be strong trust. With high trust, you will have a more effective board—one where the good qualities of each board member can build upon each other. Conversely, if the company does not properly orient and educate its board members, board trust, performance, and subsequently, company performance will suffer. You want all board members to be knowledgeable about your industry and company including its purpose, mission, values, strategic plan, policies, financials, management, culture, and the like.

Besides knowing the business, new board members need to know the other board members, and the board constitution, expectations, roles, procedures, governance requirements, performance evaluation procedures, and the like. This knowledge helps to build trust—an essential ingredient of a successful board.

Prior to their first board meeting, you should provide new board members with a thorough in-person orientation to your business. A good time for conducting the orientation and training session is within a month before the first board meeting. That will enable the new board member to put into action what is learned in the session. There may be less "Teflon learning" (more of the training will stick). Creating an open, trusting environment during new board member orientation and training will facilitate a positive learning experience.

It is suggested that you have an informal dinner with new board members the night before their first board meeting. At a minimum, call each new board member *before* the first few board meetings. Ask if there are any questions, suggestions or comments. Likewise, you may want to place a call *after* the first few board meetings. Ask how the meetings went. It is better to check in to see how the new board members are doing, rather than assume they are off to a good start.

A typical new board member orientation and training agenda is shown below and provided in Appendix 4. It is designed to impart a lot of key information in a short period of time. Start by reviewing the board's Statement of Purpose and board constitution to ensure that there is complete clarity on expectations. During the review of the constitution is a good time to reinforce the importance of keeping all discussions in confidence.

Peak-Performance, Inc. Board Member Orientation & Training Agenda

May 7, 2005

8:30   *Introduction to Company (CEO)*
- *Review Board Statement of Purpose*
- *Review Board Constitution*
- *Review Code of Conduct and Ethics (Confidentiality)*
- *Introduce Key Managers (see bios sent with orientation package)*

9:15   *Tour (CEO)*
- *Overall Headquarters*
- *Marketing & Sales*
- *Operations*
- *Product Development*
- *Finance*
- *Customer Care Center*

10:00 Break

10:15 Review of Strategic Plan (CEO)
- *Purpose, Mission, and Core Values*
- *SWOTS*
- *Unique Business Model*
- *Key Strategic Initiatives*
- *Objectives and Goals*
- *Measures, Benchmarks and Action Plans (Balanced Scorecard)*
- *Questions?*

12:15 Lunch
- *CFO (Claire Voyant) and EVP Product Development (John Gadget) will join us*

1:00 Financial Orientation (Claire Voyant)
- *Historical (balance sheet, income statement)*
- *Projections (balance sheet, income statement, cash flows)*
- *Questions?*

2:15 Wrap Up (CEO)
- *Questions and Suggestions?*

Share Relevant Information

Your goal should be to help new members quickly grasp what your business is and how it fits within the marketplace (framed within the competitive landscape). Share what you see are the key opportunities and challenges of the business. As background information, it may be helpful to cover the company's history, milestones, and organizational structure. Include brief biographies or résumés on the executive team. Provide biographies on the other board members too. You may also want to share prior board, sales, and marketing materials. In summary, share information that will be useful to the new board members. A lot of the above information can be sent in advance of the session so that the new board members can come up to speed quicker.

Focus on Your Plan

Spend a reasonable amount of time on your strategic plan (including the financials and the important issues that you need help with). The new board members should take home a clear picture of the company's future state you envision and what you deem to be the current best path to get there.

Introduce Key Personnel

Board members may provide a unique, objective perspective on your top employees. What's more, the board may need to have access to your senior managers. Thus, it is a good idea to introduce your executive team during the new board member orientation and training session.

Tour Your Facilities

There is no substitute for seeing firsthand the operations of a business. If time permits, you should include a tour of your operations as part of the new board member orientation. The sample agenda shown above and in Appendix 4 has the tour scheduled early in the orientation session. This provides new board members with a quick lay of the land. It also provides a reference point for later discussions.

Provide a Board Fact Book

When the author worked at Procter & Gamble, one of the great organizational tools that every brand manager carried with him or her was the "Fact Book." Inside the tabbed three-ring binder were the important plans about the business. Relevant business facts were also available at your fingertips (hence the name Fact Book).

This same idea can be used to help orient and train your board. A digital version can also be created and downloaded on a disk.

However, if this is done, make sure proper safeguards are in place to protect the information.

Send the Board Fact Book (or digital information) prior to the orientation and training session. This will help familiarize new board members with the company beforehand. A sample of the table of contents of Peak-Performance, Inc.'s Board Fact Book is shown below in Exhibit 7. Use this as a guide. Add or subtract whatever information is relevant to your business.

Exhibit 7. Board Member Fact Book

Peak-Performance, Inc.
Board Fact Book
(Amended April 2005)

TOPIC/TAB

- *Contact Information (key managers, board members, etc.)*
- *Board Meeting Dates/Calendar*
- *Board Meeting Agendas (most recent meetings)*
- *Board Reports (prior and current)*
- *Company History and Milestones*
  - *Background Information (marketing materials, media articles, industry information, trade publications)*
  - *Brief Overview of Key Competitors, Customers and Suppliers*
  - *Articles of Incorporation and Bylaws*
  - *Licenses, Patents, and Permits*
- *Company ownership (current and prior transitions)*
- *Historical Financials (include trend data and analysis of key metrics)*
- *Strategic Plan Summary*
  - *Purpose, Mission, and Core Values*
  - *SWOTS (Strengths, Weaknesses, Opportunities and Threats, summarized in order of priority)*
  - *Unique Business Model*

- ➢ *Objectives and Goals (summary)*
- ➢ *Strategies (summary)*
- ➢ *Key Measures and Benchmarks (summary)*
- ➢ *Tactics (Balanced Scorecard summary)*
- ➢ *Financial Forecast*
- ➢ *Capital Budget*
- ➢ *Organization Chart*
- ➢ *Management Biographies*
- ➢ *Human Resource Policies*
- ➢ *Code of Conduct and Ethics*
- ➢ *Board Member Biographies*
- ➢ *Board Constitution*
- ➢ *Audit Committee Charter*
- ➢ *Board Recruiting Matrix (not filled out)*
- ➢ *Board Search Description*
- ➢ *Board Member Evaluation Form*
- ➢ *Overall Board Evaluation (broken out by the 5 Steps)*
- ➢ *CEO Evaluation Form*
- ➢ *D&O Insurance Policy Overview (if applicable)*

Don't Overwhelm

A word of caution: do not inundate your new board members with too much information or too many details. Stay focused on the important strategic and policy issues. Provide time for new board members to digest the information. Lastly, provide ample opportunities for new board members to ask questions.

Use a Mentor

Another helpful tip is to ask one of your seasoned board members to serve as an interim mentor for each new board member. This can help quickly transfer knowledge. It can bring the new members up to speed faster.

Training Is Ongoing

Once the initial orientation and training session is complete, your work is not done. After the session would be a good time to call new board members and ask how the orientation and training session went. Probe to understand if they grasped the essentials. Offer to cover anything that is unclear. You may want to solicit suggestions to improve the session for future board members.

Board member orientation and training should not be a one-time activity. It is a good idea to check in periodically with board members to determine how they are doing. A tip to keep your board up to speed in your industry is to provide them with subscriptions to industry trade journals or magazines.

Here is another tip. Request that board members get involved with the company's products or services on an ongoing basis. As a real-life example, Home Depot expects its board members to visit the company's stores each year and to report on their findings. This is an excellent way to engage board members in the business. This approach can be applied to large and small businesses.

In summary, board member training is an ongoing process. Every board meeting is an opportunity to share more about the business, its challenges and opportunities. The investment in initial and ongoing board member training should pay good dividends. A well-informed board should contribute more to the company's success.

15. How to Run Highly Productive Board Meetings

"Sometimes I get the feeling that the two biggest problems in America today are making ends meet, and making meetings end."

—Robert Orben, an editor, writer, and former speechwriter for President Ford

15. How to Run Highly Productive Board Meetings

This chapter will share tips for running board meetings that flow efficiently and are effective.

Create an Atmosphere of Trust

The most important tip is to establish high trust among board members. An atmosphere of trust and candor fosters mutual respect. This, in turn, enables the positive qualities of board members to build upon each other. Your goal in every board meeting should be to create a climate where trust is high, so that communication is open. You want ideas to flow freely. Candid discussion and a healthy give-and-take are paramount to obtaining the best advice from the board.

Cutting down suggestions or severely limiting discussion are sure ways to squelch trust. You do not want to squash ideas before they have had a chance to be heard and nurtured. Being open to new possibilities, as well as dealing with facts and true realities, is essential to building trust. Listening to and acting upon the board's *good* advice is another way to show that you trust the board's advice.

First Meeting Introductions

The first time new board members get together, it is a good idea to begin the meeting with introductions. You want each board member to be comfortable and to get to know the other members. As a starting point, go around the table and let each board member give a brief overview of his or her background. Provide a sheet that lists contact information of all board members (this should be included in the Board Fact Book).

How Many Meetings?

One of the basic questions asked is, "How often should a board meet?" The board should meet at least four times a year. It should meet more frequently if there are serious business issues (up to twelve times a year, but only in rare cases). Four meetings are usually enough for a healthy company. Besides, too many meetings can force the board to move away from important strategic issues and cause it to deal with minor or less important issues.

Meetings should be set twelve months in advance. Consider doing this each quarter, reviewing a year rolling forward. Each quarter, board members should bring their calendars to the meeting. Any date that is not set within a year out in the future should be set. This subtle point helps ensure 100 percent attendance, important for maximizing board member commitment. It also provides an opportunity to confirm all four future meeting dates with every board member present.

You may want to establish a consistent date for your meetings such as a timeframe when you will have the prior quarter's financial statements ready. This will help maintain a discipline of reviewing recent financial results and projections. Regardless of which days you choose, it is essential that you make the dates work for *all members*. One hundred percent attendance is your only goal. Otherwise, board members will be left with critical gaps in understanding. Consequently, you may not glean their best wisdom, ideas, advice, or expertise. Unlike professional sports teams, there are no "substitutes" on small to midsize business boards. Every member counts. Perfect attendance is needed for maximum effectiveness.

Who Should Attend?

Besides board members, should "outsiders" (non-board members) attend the meetings? Only invite outsiders *who can add value* to board meetings. It is a mistake to invite guests who have no purpose or who cannot materially improve the outcome of the meetings.

You may want to invite members of management or others to parts of the board meetings. However, only invite guests who have *relevant* expertise specific to agenda items, such as your CFO, to explain the financials, or your head of product development to review your product strategy. Besides bringing relevant expertise, recognition is a side benefit not to be overlooked. Having managers present to the board demonstrates that they count enough in the organization to be exposed to the board.

In situations where it is known that leadership is going to be transferred in the near term (i.e. a family business from one generation to the next), it may be a good idea to invite the new leader to select board meetings (or portions of meetings). This familiarization will facilitate a smoother transition of power.

Outsiders, such as your accountants, are also appropriate to invite to portions of a board meeting, for example, when the yearly audit is reviewed. In a closely held company, you should provide time for the board to meet directly with the auditors for an unencumbered discussion of the company's financial health and possible risks. For a broadly traded public company, this kind of independence will be required (as part of the audit committee charter and meeting process). It should be standard operating procedure in a closely held business too.

Where Should You Meet?

The board meeting location is typically onsite at headquarters. Make sure the meeting room facilitates good eye contact. Seating should be comfortable. Distractions should be minimized. There should be easy access to communication aids such as computers, overhead projectors, and flip charts, as needed.

If the business has important remote locations, such as a factory, sales office, or service center, it may be beneficial to infrequently have meetings at those locations. This will enable the board to see the operations and meet the appropriate employees at those locations.

How Long Should Meetings Run?

Board meetings should be scheduled for a minimum of three hours. Any shorter, you cannot get into enough "substance." On the other hand, board meetings should not last any longer than six hours. If longer than six hours, then you are probably focusing on too many tactics and unnecessary details. An exception could be the annual strategic plan review meeting. This may require up to a full day; any longer and management has not done a good job in distilling the strategic plan review to the highest leverage opportunities and most critical challenges.

What About Emergency or Interim Meetings?

You should call emergency meetings but only if there is a dire need. Set expectations up front that these may occur. However, you do not want to have too many emergency meetings (perhaps once every few years). Otherwise, there is probably a fundamental problem with your business.

One way to quickly obtain the input of your board on an emergency or interim basis is to conduct a telephone conference board meeting. This will be easier for out-of-town members to "attend." It will help increase participation, especially when time is of the essence.

If you only have one or two priority topics to discuss or there is a long time between formal board meetings, consider a telephone conference board meeting. According to Jim Graves (former COO of J. C. Bradford and board member of various closely held businesses), *"Some of the best board meetings I have been in will tackle a single issue via a telephone board meeting. It is not hard to arrange, cuts unnecessary conversation and allows for more awareness of the company and CEO by not having such long delays between meetings."*

Dinner Pre-Meetings

During the research phase of writing this book, several successful private business board members have commented positively on the practice of having pre-meeting board dinners. These informal dinner gatherings are typically held once a year, the night before a board meeting. This is a good opportunity to build relationships, trust, and commitment among board members.

The Same Principles of Running Highly Effective Meetings Apply to Board Meetings

An essential part of Step 3 is establishing the right meeting content. Thoughtful selection of the meeting objectives improves the odds that you will leverage the collective time of all participants. Mary Shelley's quote serves as a reminder of the importance of establishing the right objectives for each board meeting: *"Nothing contributes so much to tranquilize the mind as a steady purpose—a point on which the soul may fix its intellectual eye."*

Start by pinpointing clear objectives that are tied to discernable outcomes that will make a difference in your business. Many of the board meeting objectives will naturally cascade from the strategic plan.

If you know what outcomes you would like from the board meeting, then you will craft a more effective agenda. As shown below in Exhibit 8a, the meeting objectives set forth exactly what should be accomplished among board members. There is a *"steady purpose"* that is linked to defined outcomes (and the strategic plan).

Exhibit 8a. Board Meeting Objectives Example

Peak-Performance, Inc.
Board Meeting Objectives

April 15, 2005
7:30 a.m. to 12:00 p.m.
First Floor Conference Room

- ❖ *Decide (go/no go) on pursuing southeast acquisition opportunity (board vote)*
- ❖ *Provide feedback and ideas on strategic initiatives*
  - *New Product Plan*
  - *Technology Plan*
- ❖ *Review and agree on key performance measures*
- ❖ *Vote on Bank LOC increase*
- ❖ *Preview future meetings*
  - *Generate agenda ideas*
  - *Schedule 2nd quarter '06 meeting*

Do not use board meeting time to rehash what is in your board report. As you can see in the Peak-Performance, Inc. sample agenda (see Exhibit 8b later in this chapter for a partial agenda or Appendix 5 for the full agenda), there is very little time allocated for review of tactical information. That should have been covered in the board report, which every member should have read beforehand. As shown in Peak-Performance, Inc.'s sample agenda, the board agenda should have clearly defined strategic or policy topics to cover, with associated timeframes, leaving enough time for active discussion and input from all board members.

Develop the Habit of Disciplined Preparation

Disciplined preparation is a key success factor for Step 3. Management should discipline itself to write a clear board report that covers key business information and issues. This practice helps ensure that you have thought through and are focused on the right issues. Typically, these are the areas where you need the most strategic help.

The report should include information relevant to strategic or policy discussions in the upcoming meeting and the most recent top line financials (with trend data). A summary of progress against key measures is also helpful to include in the board report. However, ultimately, the board should define what information it needs and how often it wants it.

You should present board information in a way that the board members will know what has changed since the last meeting. In essence, you want to continue the conversation from where you left off in the last meeting. Reframe the "conversation" to the present or anticipated future state of affairs. Your goal with the board report should be to provide enough understanding of the business issues at hand so that the board members will be adequately prepared for the upcoming meeting. Provide the right balance; they should not have to ask a lot of clarification questions, yet members should not be overwhelmed with too much information.

Give ample thought as to what long-term strategic or policy issues you need the most help from the board. Prepare in advance. You know when the meetings are well in advance. Hopefully, you know what the important issues are. So make the time and prepare. You will have much more effective meetings if you are disciplined and develop the habit of preparation.

Send Information in Advance

Make sure you send the agenda and board report in advance so that there is enough time for members to review and prepare. It is suggested that all information be sent so that it is *received at least one week prior to the meeting* unless there is a pressing, time-sensitive issue (for example, a pending acquisition of a business). On a related point, the expectation should be clear that every board member thoroughly reads the board report, background, and financial information ahead of time. This expectation can be set in the board roll description (see Appendix 1) and the board constitution (see Appendix 2).

Start Board Meetings on Time

It is inexcusable for board meetings to start late. The expectation that board meetings start on time should be made clear during board recruitment and during board orientation. Besides sending a signal that the business is run poorly, lateness costs everyone money. Similarly, timeframes for breaks should be adhered to. Distractions during the meeting should be minimized (i.e. cell phones turned off to prevent interruptions). Lastly, out of respect to everyone's time, you should end meetings on time.

Stick to a Strategic Agenda

There is a science and an art to successful meetings. The agenda, with its respective topics and timeframes, represents most of the science of the meeting. As shown in Exhibit 8b below, the board agenda (partial agenda is shown, Appendix 5 shows the entire agenda) should have clearly defined timeframes. Tactical items that could quickly eat up meeting time are not included on the agenda. Adequate time is allocated to each topic, depending on the complexity and importance of the outcome. You want to ensure that collective input from the different board experts is heard and integrated into the discussion and decision processes.

Put the most important items in the beginning of the agenda. People are fresh in the beginning of a meeting. Additionally, you will be less burdened with time pressures at the end of the meeting.

As you can see below, the *southeast strategic acquisition* is the first item on the Peak-Performance sample agenda. The reason it is placed first is because it is the most important strategic growth opportunity for the business. Also note that appropriate outsiders are invited to relevant parts of the meeting. For example, John Gadget, EVP of Product Development is invited for the *new products strategy* discussion so that he can add to and benefit from the discussion at hand.

Exhibit 8b. Board Agenda Example (partial)

Peak-Performance, Inc.
Board Meeting Agenda

April 15, 2005
7:30 a.m. to 12:00 p.m.
First Floor Conference Room

Specific Agenda Items and Timeframes

7:30   *Open discussion on southeast acquisition opportunity (preparation materials included in board package)*
- *How well does the prospect fit our strategy?*
- *What other opportunities/risks do you see?*
- *How is the cultural fit?*
- *Other suggestions, issues, or concerns?*
- *Vote on pursuing acquisition or not (pending board discussion—written resolution included with board package)*

9:30   *Break*

9:45   *Introduction to New Products Strategy and John Gadget (EVP Product Development)*
- *New Products Presentation by John Gadget, EVP of Product Development (please review New Product Plan and John's bio in board report)*
- *Q & A of John Gadget from board*
- *Board reactions to presentation and suggestions/builds on Peak-Performance New Product Plan*

10:45 *Strategic Thought Starter Discussion: "What is the company's plan to take advantage of new technology?"*
- *Do we have a good handle on the available technologies that can help our company grow?*

- *If not, how are we going to obtain them?*
- *What kind of ROI are we realizing from investments in technology?*
- *Reactions/suggestions to improve Technology Plan (included in board package)*
- *Networking opportunities—Does the board know of good technology strategy consultants?*

The art of meeting management comes into play by diplomatically keeping everyone focused on the topic at hand while fostering an environment where disagreement and truth are respected and maximum input is gleaned from all members.

Do not get distracted by unimportant diversions. Control the meeting (one of the board chair's responsibilities). Ensure everyone sticks to the strategy and policy items on the agenda. Summarize what board members are saying to keep things moving forward and to signal to members that they have been heard and understood. Correct or clarify any misunderstandings.

When a topic is presented during the board meeting, the chair should explicitly state what outcome he or she wants from the board members. The meeting objectives form the basis of this. Is the topic just an update, or is it a problem you need help solving, or does it require a decision (vote)? Regardless of what the topic is, it is important to clarify what you want the board to do (listen, suggest ideas, solve problems, decide, vote, etc.).

If new ideas are brought forth that are off topic, make a list on a wipe board or notepad. These ideas can be discussed at the end of the meeting (pending available time) or during a future meeting, if warranted.

Avoid Groupthink

As mentioned, part of the art of meeting management is to foster an atmosphere where open dissent and the challenging of ideas are welcome. Any subject should be fair game to discuss. However, all topics should be placed on the agenda beforehand. If disagreements occur among board members, they should be respected. Encouraging different points of view is critical to building and maintaining trust and to coming up with better ideas and solutions. Candor should rule the day. The chair (or CEO) wants to create healthy respect among all board members and to avoid groupthink.

Establish a Clear Voting Process

Many board topics do not require a vote. However, for a statutory board, if there is a decision that the board is acting upon, a formal voting process should be followed. Of note, a formal voting process is not recommended for an advisory board. If an advisory board is asked to formally vote, it could be deemed to be acting more like a statutory board. Avoid this potential risk. This does not mean you cannot informally ask advisory board members to say what their preferences are. On the contrary, you should ask them to tell you what they would recommend on any given topic. Just do not record there opinion as an official "vote."

Most statuary board topics, actions, or resolutions requiring a vote should start with an open discussion. After the open discussion, the board chair generally calls for a motion. Specifically, the chair asks for a volunteer to make a motion for approval (or one has already been put forth prior to the meeting in writing and is handed out during the meeting). If the first motion for approval is made, the chair then asks for a second to approve the motion. Objections are usually considered and discussion ensues, if any. The process continues with a summary of all those in favor and all those opposed to the motion. The vote is concluded with a declaration that the motion has been accepted or rejected, contingent upon the outcome of the vote.

Document Key Discussion Points and Next Steps

All of the statuary board voting topics, actions, or resolutions should be recorded in writing, usually by the secretary. These should be incorporated into the minutes of the board meeting. It is also a good idea to have your attorney copied on the minutes. This improves communication. It also serves to minimize legal concerns or liability issues that can arise from miscommunication. For an advisory board that probably does not have an official secretary, you may want to have an executive assistant attend the advisory board meetings to take notes. This will enable you to focus on asking the right questions and listening instead of taking notes. However, only do this if you can trust the person to keep confidences and it is not awkward for either party.

Unfortunately, many board meetings conclude without clear action plans. Part of the problem is that the next steps are not captured and documented. Often, this leads to inaction. At the conclusion of every board meeting, there should be a written action plan summary of who should do what and when it will be done. Establish clear next steps with responsibility for actions and timeframes. Documentation aids memory. It also improves accountability and performance.

(Step 4)
THE RIGHT BOARD FOCUS

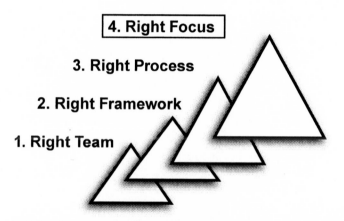

4. Right Focus

3. Right Process

2. Right Framework

1. Right Team

This section covers Step 4, The Right Focus. It reflects the leadership aspects of a board (strategically, doing the right things). The first chapter describes effective ways to consistently keep a high-leverage strategic focus in board discussions. This is done in part through *The 15 Key Strategic Questions* every business should ask. Tips on listening, another important aspect of effective board leadership, are shared in a separate chapter.

16. How to Stay Focused On Winning Strategies (The 15 Key Strategic Questions)

"The significant problems we face today cannot be solved at the same level of thinking we were at when we created them."

—Albert Einstein, a Nobel Peace Prize-winning German-American physicist best known for his theories on relativity

16. How to Stay Focused On Winning Strategies (The 15 Key Strategic Questions)

Asking the right questions and ensuring that the right answers are given are two of the most important responsibilities of a board chair and the board as a whole. It is the foundation of good corporate governance and the essence of true leadership. This chapter shows you how to stay focused on winning strategies during board meetings. The key to accomplishing this is asking the right strategic questions. Some of the questions are simple. Thus, they often do not get asked during board meetings. However, simple questions can sometimes provide profound answers.

Focus on the Big Picture

Every board meeting should have considerable time dedicated on the agenda to discuss important strategy or policy issues. Obviously, the strategic plan satisfies this need. However, focused strategic discussion usually occurs during one meeting each year.

A suggestion to keep strategy and policy the prime focus of the board's attention and interest is to have at least one strategic discussion topic during *every* meeting. A board can usually provide the most help if it concentrates on the big-picture issues and choices. Strategy is about choice. It is just as much about inclusion (what you choose to do) as it is about exclusion (what you choose *not* to do). It is about making the right choices to achieve the long-term mission, objectives, and goals of the business. Assuming that the business leaders and board understand what the long-term outcomes of the business are, asking the right strategic questions of the board will help uncover the right options and choices to achieve those long-term plans. Using The 15 Key Strategic Questions (which are discussed below) is an excellent way to facilitate those discussions.

The 15 Key Strategic Questions

Exhibit 9, below lists *The 15 Key Strategic Questions (Questions)*. They serve as "strategic thought starters" for board meetings and strategic planning sessions. The *Questions* focus board meeting attention on the "right things." They will help you to excel in Step 4 *(Right Focus)*. They are also designed to help the company understand what it should be doing. Just as important, they will help the company learn what it does not know and what it should know.

Each of the fifteen *Questions* starts with a topic overview question centered on an important issue (e.g. important customers, how the company invents, and the like). This topic overview question helps define the current state of affairs in the business. It is followed with a series of related questions that help sort out what the best paths (choices) should be with respect to a desired future state. In effect, the *Questions* challenge management and the board to improve the business from a high leverage vantage point.

Here are a few tips on how to get the most from the board out of the *Questions*. First, choose at least one *Question* to discuss during every board meeting. If you recall from Chapter 15 *(How to Run Highly Productive Board Meetings),* the sample agenda from Peak-Performance, Inc. had a series of technology questions on the agenda. These are from question number 12 *(The Technology Question)*.

10:45 Strategic Thought Starter Discussion: "What is the company's plan to take advantage of new technology?"
- ***Do we have a good handle on the available technologies that can help our company grow?***
- ***If not, how are we going to obtain them?***
- ***What kind of ROI are we realizing from investments in technology?***
- ***Reactions/suggestions to improve Technology Plan (included in board package)***
- ***Networking opportunities—Does the board know of good technology strategy consultants?***

Second, it is always a good idea to ask board members to suggest which *Question* should be worked on during the next board meeting. Oftentimes, they have an objective and unfiltered view as to what the right issues are.

Third, have the board and the executive team sort through the most relevant *Questions* to ask during the annual strategic planning meeting. Lastly, several of the *Questions* should be asked periodically as circumstances change. Thus, the answers are likely to change as well.

Each and every *Question* is relevant to any business, regardless of size, industry, or stage in life cycle. The *15 Key Strategic Questions* can be modified to your company situation or you can add questions that may be more relevant or specific to your business needs. The important point is to ask the right questions in board meetings so that the company and the board are focused on the highest leverage opportunities that will help the company win (grow and earn more profit than the competition).

Exhibit 9. The *Fifteen Key Strategic Questions*

---

1. <u>**The Fundamental Question**</u> — **Should we be in this business?**
   - ➤ Do we have a meaningful purpose and mission?
   - ➤ Are there any businesses, plants, divisions, or sub-areas of the company that we would not be in if we started them from scratch today?
   - ➤ Can we identify our mediocre or unprofitable businesses and should we exit them?
   - ➤ If we are unsure, what is our plan to be able to answer these questions?

2. <u>**The Team Question**</u>—**Do we have *all* of the *right* players on the team?**
   - ➤ If we do not have all of the right players, how and when are we going to obtain them?

> ➢ If we have the right players, are they in the right positions?
> ➢ What employees, if any, are holding the company back?
> ➢ How and when are we going to transition to the right team?

3. **The Unique Business Model Question (UBM) — What *unique* aspect of the business gives us a reason to win (grow and earn more profit than the competition)?** Here is a more elaborate definition of a Unique Business Model: *A Unique Business Model is a concentrated advantage (high leverage) that the company does better than anyone else, is unique and meaningful to customers, and is defendable against competition.*

There are three "C's" or success ingredients of a good UBM. Specifically, a good UBM is: 1) a concentrated advantage; 2) customer-centered; and 3) competitively positioned.

Concentrated Advantage — The first "C" of a good UBM is based upon a fundamental principle of success. That is, to be successful, it is a good idea to have your forces *concentrated* so that you gain an advantage over competitors. In business, as in warfare, you cannot attack or defend everywhere. As Frederick the Great said, "He who attempts to defend everywhere defends nothing."

Customer-Centered — The second "C" of a good UBM is that it focuses externally on *customer* perceptions of value versus internal company perceptions. The competitive battleground of business is ultimately won or lost in the customer's mind. Every company's success is linked to how well it provides value to customers relative to other choices they have.

Competitively Positioned — The third "C" of a good UBM is that it must be defendable against *competition*. The UBM should impose meaningful barriers-to-entry. It is no use developing a UBM that competitors can easily duplicate. When you look at truly successful companies, they all have an underlying

UBM that provides an advantage that is difficult to attack; it is defendable.

Below are a series of questions that should be asked in sequence. These questions can help a company and board to discover a good UBM for the business.

➢ What are concentrated advantages (important strengths, competencies, or expertise) that the company currently has?

➢ What are concentrated advantages (important strengths, competencies, or expertise) that the company can obtain in the future?

➢ Which of the above concentrated advantages are customer-centered (advantages that are relevant in the minds of current and prospective customers)?

➢ Which of the above are unique?

➢ Which of the above are defendable against competition?

➢ Which of the above is the company's *highest-leverage* opportunity to grow and win?

➢ Do we have enough influence or control over the outcomes if we leverage the UBM?

➢ How can we best capitalize on the UBM?

➢ How do our development plans build upon and align with the UBM?

4. **The Customer Question — Does the company have the right customers?**

➢ Who are our best customers? Consider the 80:20 Rule and realize that it applies to customers.

➢ How is our business trending with our best customers?

➢ Should any customers be added *or dropped?*

➢ Do we know what the company's real customer needs are? If not, how can we learn what they really are? If so, how can we do a better job of meeting or exceeding those needs?

5. **The Invention Question—Are we inventing the right things to maximize success?** The Invention Question should apply to many areas of the business such as product development,

operations, capital fulfillment, human resources, marketing, and the like.

➤ How does the company invent?

➤ What are our invention or improvement plans?

➤ Are we inventing in the right areas of the business?

6 The Learning Question—How can the company learn better?

➤ Does the company maximize its learning opportunities?

➤ Are we maximizing what we learn from competition?

➤ Are we maximizing what we learn from customers?

➤ Are we maximizing what we learn from suppliers?

➤ Are we tapped into the right experts to help us learn efficiently?

➤ How can we cost-effectively accelerate learning in our company?

7. The Culture Question — What is the company's culture and is it appropriate?

➤ If appropriate, how can we leverage it better?

➤ If not appropriate, what is the right culture? How are we going to obtain it?

➤ What are the key areas of the company's culture that we should protect?

➤ Does the company have the right values?

➤ Are they understood and leveraged throughout the company?

8. The Scorecard Question — What measures of greatness does the company want to achieve? The board should focus this question on long-term objectives and goals.

➤ What are the company's measurement systems?

➤ Does the company have the right measures?

➤ Are they reliable and useful?

➤ Is the company using those measures for maximum advantage?

➤ Are they understood and aligned throughout the company?

➢ How well do the company's key metrics benchmark against competition?

9. **The Cash Question—Does the company have the right cash flows to achieve its objectives?** This question is critical to understand for start-up companies.
   ➢ What are the company's cash flow and capital needs?
   ➢ How can they best be satisfied?
   ➢ How are those needs projected to change over time?
   ➢ Are they proactively managed?

10. **The Policies Question—Does the company have the appropriate business policies in place?**
    ➢ What are the company's material employment policies (employment at will, sexual harassment, anti-discrimination policies, and the like) and are they appropriate and understood?
    ➢ How do we know that they are appropriate and understood?
    ➢ Are they adequate and appropriate for the size and life cycle of the company?
    ➢ What is the company's communications policy?
    ➢ Is the company's communications policy effective?
    ➢ How do we know that the company's communications policy is effective?
    ➢ How can it be improved?

11. **The Internal Control Question — Does the company have the right internal controls in place?**
    ➢ What are the company's internal control policies?
    ➢ Are they appropriate (too much control, too little control)?
    ➢ Are they aligned with the purpose, mission, and values?
    ➢ Are they reliable and accurate?
    ➢ Are they cost-effective?
    ➢ How can they be improved?

12. **The Technology Question — What is the company's plan to take advantage of new technology?**
    ➢ Do we have a good handle on the available technologies that can help our company grow?
    ➢ If not, how are we going to obtain them?
    ➢ What kind of ROI are we realizing from investments in technology?

13. **The Risk Question — What are the greatest risks facing the company?**
    ➢ Have we properly identified the key risks?
    ➢ What can be done to minimize those risks?
    ➢ What is the company's appetite for risk? Of note, the company's ability to take on risk is important to know as potential solutions are considered.
    ➢ Is the company appropriately diversified on a product, customer, and supplier basis? If not, how is it going to become diversified?

14. **The Life Cycle Question—Is the company maximizing its portfolio of products or services according to their life cycle stage?**
    ➢ What is the life cycle of the company's key products or services? Are they different?
    ➢ What life cycle stage is each product or service in?
    ➢ Is the company investing appropriately based upon the life cycle stage of each product or service?

15. **The Exit Question — What is the company's current exit plan?**
    ➢ How will it best be realized to maximize shareholder return?
    ➢ When is the optimal time to sell or transition leadership?
    ➢ Does the company have a solid plan for succession?
    ➢ Is there a crisis succession plan in place?

17. The Lost Art of Listening

*"When I listen I have the power, when I talk
I give it away."*

—Voltaire, one of France's greatest authors
and philosophers, who preached the value
of freedom of thought

17. The Lost Art of Listening

Ask, Then *Listen*!

Rene McPherson (board of director positions have included Mercantile Stores, Dow Jones, Milliken, and Westinghouse) shared a great tip. Specifically, he said (paraphrased) to: "Continually use the four magic words and ask, *what do you think?"* Rene then advised to listen to the board's feedback and be prepared to act upon the board's good advice.

As we saw in Chapter 16 (illustrated with *The 15 Key Strategic Questions*), one of the best ways to ensure the right focus is to ask the right questions. Asking the right questions focuses board discussions on the most important topics. However, to be truly effective, it is important to listen and be willing to change your position based on what you hear from board members. Active listening should be your goal in every board meeting. Unfortunately, it is becoming a lost art. You want to harness quality, expert advice and glean a *realistic* picture of the business and its opportunities and risks. You *cannot* do this well if you spend most of the board meeting talking.

The 20:80 Listening Rule

A good guideline is to apply the 20:80 Listening Rule. In board meetings, the chair and all of the board members should speak no more than 20 percent of the time. Each board member should *listen* during the remaining 80 percent of time. The chair should always be receptive to all board members' input. He or she should look to modify or even completely change paths for better opportunities if they are presented by the board members.

It is a good idea to listen to the feelings as well as the words. Pay attention to body language. Tone of voice is important too. Try to understand the emotions as well as the logic behind the board's comments and suggestions.

Are You Mentally Tired?

After a board meeting, there is a good indicator of how well you have listened. Are you *mentally tired?* Attentive listening is a mental workout. However, when it comes to effective board meetings, it is worth the "mind sweat."

Probe for Clarity

Use of a second set of four magic words, *"say more about that"* is very appropriate when someone tosses out a comment that is not understood. Too often the board chair and/or members do not clarify what is said. This can lead to misperceptions or lost opportunities.

For the most important strategic or policy topics, make sure input is obtained from *all* board members. Listen to everyone's point of view or suggestions, especially if they are different. An effective way to do this is to go around the table and ask each board member, in turn, "What do you think, (name)?" Encourage dissenting points of view, as long as they are well reasoned. Probe and challenge the board until you get the input and advice you need. Board members should leave the board meeting having gone through a rigorous mental workout too.

Here's another tip: It is good practice to check for accuracy of what you heard. Periodically paraphrase and summarize key discussions. This will also help the secretary capture the important points of the meeting for the minutes, summary, and follow-up action steps.

Consider an "Open-Door" Communications Policy

You may want to consider an unfiltered listening tool such as an "open-door" communications policy between board members and the leaders of the company. This may enable the company to discover hidden areas of concern or opportunities for improvement. Specifically, board members would be encouraged to communicate directly with management or the executive team. Sometimes board members can listen in a more effective way than the CEO.

Of note, the purpose of an open-door communications channel is to find truth in an atmosphere of trust. It is not to create side conversations where trust among the board and the CEO can be tarnished. Trust is critical to a board's success. It is hard to earn and fragile to maintain. If either the board or the CEO violates trust by compromising an open-door communications policy, the board's performance will suffer.

If the board uses direct contact with management to check up on the CEO without his or her prior knowledge, this can greatly compromise trust between the board and the CEO. Likewise, in situations when the board uncovers and reports a problem, it is essential that the CEO accepts the news openly and acts upon it in good faith with the goal to improve the business. Otherwise, if there is a witch hunt after bad news is shared, future feedback will not occur. Employees need to feel that feedback will be treated without retaliation. After all, it is better to learn of problems from within the company instead of from customers or competitors.

Not All Advice Is Good

Thom Gerdes, CEO of Plastic Moldings LLC, advises *"to recognize that only the CEO and leadership team of an organization can make final decisions on the appropriate course of action for a business."* Board members bring valuable experience and expertise. However, they may not have the "full perspective" on an issue. Further, not *all* board advice is good, relevant, or appropriate. In addition, it is not unusual to obtain conflicting advice among board members. This can be healthy. However, if there is conflicting advice, it is prudent to distinguish between fact and opinion. Separate emotions, judgment, and opinions from facts.

Sometimes, there are not many facts. Other times, there is limited time to obtain them. In those situations, good judgment will be needed to make a decision. That is OK. The point is to understand the differences between fact and opinion when making a decision.

Good CEOs should use many sources of advice, including the board, outside professionals, the leadership team, customers, suppliers, consultants, peer learning groups, and reading, among others. Careful consideration of relevant advice will result in better decisions and a more successful business when used honestly in reflection of your own insights.

Communicate Frequently

Sharing information builds trust. As already discussed, it is important to document ideas, suggestions, agreements, and key action steps. Send summary reports *promptly* after meetings to all board members. Another communications opportunity that is often overlooked is to provide periodic updates outside of board meetings. Here is a caution, though: do not overwhelm board members with too much information. You may want to send monthly top-line financials (with trends) and summaries of key business measures to each board member. A good board should be trusted. Besides, they need factual information to provide valid advice.

E-mail is an easy method to update the board. It can ensure that strategic developments and policy issues are shared efficiently and on a timely basis with all members.

Do not be bashful. Have informal breakfast or lunch meetings or use the phone to solicit board member feedback from time to time. They are there to help. At a minimum, the CEO should have one-on-one discussions at least once a year with each board member. These meetings are helpful to uncover feedback or issues that a board member may not want to discuss in a group setting.

(Step 5)
THE RIGHT BOARD IMPROVEMENT

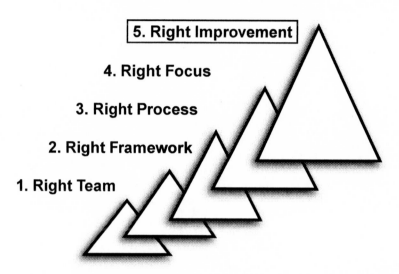

5. Right Improvement

4. Right Focus

3. Right Process

2. Right Framework

1. Right Team

This section covers the last step to a peak-performing board. Specifically, it concentrates on measuring performance so that purposeful improvement can occur. Based on survey research, it was surprising to find out that very few small to midsize companies formally measure overall board performance. It is essential that performance measures be taken in order to have purposeful improvement plans. There are useful examples on how to evaluate individual board members, the overall board, and the CEO. These evaluations lay the foundation for continual board improvement— the essence of Step 5.

18 How to Evaluate and Improve Board Effectiveness

"Well done is better than well said."

—Benjamin Franklin, a leading American statesperson, inventor, philanthropist, publisher, and revolutionary

18. How to Evaluate and Improve Board Effectiveness

Very Few Evaluate Board Performance

Not many companies have a formal process in place to evaluate the effectiveness of the board. Specifically, based upon the Board Governance Survey that was conducted by the author, *less than 8 percent* of small to midsize companies claimed that they had a formal process in place to evaluate individual board member effectiveness. Just as concerning is the fact that over 30 percent of companies surveyed claimed they had board members who were not performing as well as they would like.

Board Members Favor Evaluations

Similar to any employee or corporate asset, you want to ensure that the board is providing the best return. Boards and board members are no different. While board member evaluations may be perceived to be a sensitive issue, according to a National Association of Corporate Directors (NACD) survey *(2001-2002 Public Governance Survey)*, 91 percent of board members claim to be in favor of regular evaluations.

Reviewing Performance Linked to Board Success

One of the best ways to achieve a peak-performing board is through the recruiting process (Step 1: *Right Team*). However, no one is perfect and everyone can improve. Thus, it is prudent to periodically review your board's performance. This includes the individual member's performance and the board as a whole. As the research has shown, the measurement process of Step 5 *(Right Improvement)* is rarely taken. That is unfortunate. It is difficult, if not impossible, to improve if you do not have an accurate assessment of how well you are performing.

Board members and boards that are evaluated will likely be more effective than those that are not, assuming the evaluation process is fair, done properly, and improvement plans are acted upon. Research conducted by the author supports this opinion. Specifically, companies that conducted formal evaluations of their boards claimed to have higher overall board performance ratings as shown in the chart below:

Company Response	Overall Board Rating
Conduct Formal Evaluation: "Yes"	**8.8**
Conduct Formal Evaluation: "No"	**6.8**
Based on a Board Governance Survey conducted in August 2004 using a ten-point scale where 10 = "highly effective" and 1 = "not effective." $n = 112$	

The survey results net out to a 29 percent higher overall board rating for companies that conducted formal board evaluations versus those that did not. As a side benefit, evaluations help instill accountability into the company's culture. Board evaluations signal that the company wants to objectively improve performance.

Start Slow

Since board performance evaluations are uncommon, it may be beneficial to wade your way into formal performance evaluations. One tip is to start with an informal but purposeful open-ended discussion of the board's performance. This discussion should conclude with specific next steps on how the board can perform better in the future. After this initial discussion, it is recommended that more formal performance evaluations are conducted. The goal is to reach a point where formal written evaluations are conducted periodically that evaluate measurable contributions from the overall board and its members. More specifics on how to accomplish this are discussed below.

Periodic Evaluations Are Recommended

This chapter begins with individual board member evaluations. It concludes with the overall board evaluation. Both are important steps to board success.

It is recommended that individual member and overall board reviews be done periodically, ideally every year. At a minimum, individual board member evaluations should be done before term limits expire. For instance, if the board constitution stipulates a three-year renewable term, it would make sense to conduct at least one board member performance evaluation *before* the term expires. The evaluation should be done well before term expiration so that the board member has a chance to correct any performance issues that may surface in the evaluation.

While requiring more time, annual evaluations are a good practice to follow. They will make it easier to improve the board if it is not performing optimally. Additionally, an annual review will provide more opportunities to recognize a great board (or individual board members). Lastly, if there are performance issues, there is a better chance they will be addressed and corrected.

Let's take a look at how to conduct effective individual board member evaluations. Later on, we will discuss the overall board evaluation process.

How to Evaluate Individual Board Members

The Board Governance Survey revealed that over 30 percent of companies surveyed claimed they had board members who were not performing up to standards. One of the worst things you can do to tarnish a board's effectiveness is to let a poor-performing member remain on the board. From a psychological perspective, this can bring down higher-performing members. Pragmatically, a poor-performing board member is similar to cancer. It should be removed quickly.

Realize that no one has a 1.000 batting average. Unfortunately, a poor-performing board member may need to be dismissed. This situation can be difficult. It requires good interpersonal skills. However, it is much easier if an effective and fair evaluation process is in place. What's more, if the evaluation is done right, it can sometimes prevent a board member from sliding down a slippery slope of poor performance.

Individual evaluations can be done through an informal or formal process. However, they should be done. Most confident board members will not object. To the contrary, they usually will be glad to take part in evaluations, as long as they are reasonably fair and based on a logical foundation from which to evaluate and improve performance.

Setting clear expectations is the first step in the board member evaluation process. When you recruit board members, it is best to set the expectation that evaluations will be conducted. Even better, explain the success criteria (see the Board Search Description in Appendix 1). This will help improve acceptance of this atypical step towards board success.

During the board orientation is a good time to cover how a board member will be evaluated, what the success criteria are, and on what terms he or she can or should be removed. Ultimately, if the business is not doing well over time, the board, the chair, and/or the CEO should be removed.

Use an Evaluation Form

It is best to do individual member evaluations in writing. You will find a simple, easy-to-use board member evaluation form in Appendix 6. An excerpt of the evaluation form is shown below in Exhibit 10 (Appendix 6 shows the complete evaluation form). It is for a self-assessment. The evaluation form can be adapted to other forms of evaluation, for example, a mutual evaluation where both the CEO and the board member do an evaluation, or board members evaluate each other. Additional evaluation processes will be discussed later in this chapter.

As you can see on the evaluation form, the board member is rated on a scale from one (poor/weak) to ten (excellent/peak) for each evaluation criterion. The evaluation form is easy to fill out. It should take *no more than thirty minutes* per board member to complete. A check mark is placed in the appropriate column contingent upon the board member's performance. There is also space to add written comments on the back, as appropriate. This enables the evaluator to go into more depth and provide specific feedback.

Inspect What You Expect

The criteria provided in the evaluations should be adapted to your own business and board needs. For example, if you have a family business, you may want to include a criterion such as "sensitivity to family member needs." The importance of this criterion to a family business will be discussed in Chapter 20 *(Family Board Matters)*. It is suggested that you only include the most important measures of performance—ones that tell the true test of success. Profitability should be among them.

By design, all evaluation criteria closely parallel the expectations set forth in the board constitution and description of what great board members do. This consistency and linkage helps ensure alignment. It also improves the likelihood that you retain the right board experts and that they will perform as you expect.

Exhibit 10. Board Member Evaluation Form (partial)

Peak-Performance, Inc. Board Member Effectiveness Evaluation

Board Member's Name:
Date of Evaluation:
Evaluation Period (from, to):
Evaluator's Name (and signature):

Evaluation Criteria	Weak (Poor)			Meets (Satisfactory)				Peak (Excellent)		
	1	2	3	4	5	6	7	8	9	10
1. Focuses On Strategy/Policy										
2. Helps Invent										
3. Provides Expert Advice										
4. Knowledge of Business										
5. Preparation/Attendance/Punctuality										
6. Initiative (Proactive)										
7. Integrity/Confidentiality										
8. Participation (Balanced)										
9. Works Well With Others										
10. Overall Evaluation										

No performance appraisal method is completely objective or accurate. That's because it is too difficult to quantify all of the attributes, variations, motivations, and outcomes of human performance. However, using some form of quasi-objective assessment is the only way to purposefully improve performance. To illustrate this point, imagine you are the batting coach of a professional baseball team. Your goal is to improve the team's batting average, yet you do not have data on any of your players' batting performance. Trying to evaluate and improve each player's batting performance without batting averages and other performance measures such as strikeouts, walks, runs, RBIs, and the like would be very difficult. There is no objective way to determine a player's performance or opportunities for improvement without appropriate data. The same is true for board members. Thus, while not perfect, board member evaluations are a reasonable tool to help you determine then purposefully improve board member performance. As mentioned earlier, there are several different approaches or options for conducting individual board member evaluations. They are discussed in the paragraphs that follow.

Option One: Self-Assessment

Recognizing that board evaluations are not the norm in small to midsize companies and they may be uncomfortable to administer at first, there are three suggested approaches to consider. Each has a different level of threat or intrusiveness. The first and least threatening approach is to have each board member do a self-assessment. To conduct a self-assessment, it is recommended that a board evaluation form (shown in Appendix 6), or an adaptation of it be used. Have each board member independently check off (using the ten-point scale) how they believe they are performing in each of the respective areas. This self-evaluation is the least threatening because the board member does his or her own appraisal of performance. In most cases, you will obtain a reasonably good assessment of the board member's performance. This is particularly true if the board has recruited the members who are on the board for the right reasons. At a minimum, you will learn how each board member perceives his or her respective performance.

Option Two: Chair/CEO Evaluates

The second option is to have the chair (or CEO, if in that role) conduct evaluations for each board member. This is consistent with typical employee performance appraisal practices. It can be perceived to be more threatening than a self-evaluation (option one) and judgmentally, it is not as fair and accurate as a mutual evaluation (option three). However, it should be more beneficial than not doing any evaluation. At least there will be thought given to board member performance and improvement on a regular basis.

Option Three: Mutual Evaluations

This method is the most objective and fair approach. However, it is the most time-consuming. It is suggested that both the chair and board member complete separate board member evaluation forms on that member. This evaluation process will likely result in a more complete and accurate board member evaluation, since both parties input is considered. It also enables both parties to be heard. Finally, it should help address performance misperceptions that sometimes occur.

Another twist on mutual evaluations is to have each board member evaluate each of the other board members. One of the experienced board members that the author interviewed during the research phase of the book shared a situation where this was done. The board was large (eleven members). It had one member who consistently had to prove how smart he was. As such, he monopolized meeting time and squelched other members from being heard. During the mutual evaluation process, board members complained about this "I am smart" behavior. In fact, several board members seriously considered resigning if the problem was not resolved. It is less likely the problem would have surfaced without a mutual evaluation process among board members.

Provide Individual Feedback

Board member performance should be evaluated yearly using the same criteria (assuming it remains relevant). After the evaluations are complete, the chair (if there is one) or CEO (if there is no chair) should meet with each board member individually to review and discuss the results. If the results are poor, especially from both parties' perspective (assuming there was a mutual evaluation), then the next step should be clear. The discussion should be kept on a professional and unemotional level. The review should be the focal point. The board member should be asked for reactions. Usually, the next steps emerge from the conversation, especially if performance expectations and outcomes were set during the recruiting and orientation processes. On a related point, it is worthwhile to review Step 1 *(Right Team)*. See if there is an area that can be improved in the identification and recruiting process. Can you identify what went wrong and why it went wrong?

If the results are mediocre, the next steps are not as clear. Ideally, the board member evaluation form will point the direction for areas to improve. The review discussion should focus on those areas. It should conclude with concrete action steps to improve the board member's performance.

If the results are exceptional, the next steps are easy. The board member should be properly recognized with true appreciation for his or her specific contributions.

The Overall Board Evaluation

Now that we have reviewed how to conduct an individual board member evaluation, let's look at an Overall Board Evaluation (OBE) form (shown in Appendix 7). In a nutshell, an OBE is a diagnostic tool. It assesses how well the board is doing in each of the 5 Steps and what the business results are. Specifically, the OBE determines if the board:

➤ Has the right team (Step 1);
➤ Has the right framework (Step 2);
➤ Has the right processes in place (Step 3);
➤ Has the right focus (Step 4);
➤ Has the right evaluation and improvement (Step 5); and
➤ Is generating the right results for the business. This reflects the output of all the 5 Steps.

A board's overall performance can be categorized into three general levels of performance. They are represented in the triangle below. The names of each clearly describe the board's overall performance level: "peak"; "meets"; or "weak."

Three Levels of Overall Board Performance

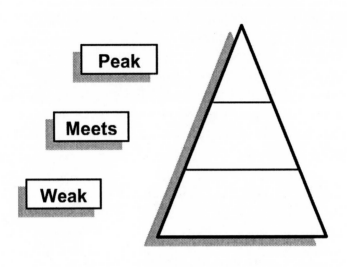

Peak Performance

The highest level, "peak-performance," is at the top of the triangle. It occurs when the board has near mastery of the 5 Steps. Board members are consistently of high quality. Board performance is enhanced from a team of experts. There is a higher ratio of independent (outside) to inside members. There is a balanced and complementary level of expertise represented on the board. The whole is greater than the sum of its parts.

Trust is very high. There is excellent chemistry and mutual respect among board members. Ideas and suggestions flow freely. Virtually any company issue is fair game for discussion. Board members take a dissenting position when necessary. There is disciplined preparation and follow-up to board meetings. The executive team promptly acts upon the board's *good* suggestions and advice. The board works on a highly strategic level. It rarely, if ever, spends time on tactics.

Preparation among all board members is thorough. There is 100 percent participation in virtually every meeting. Board members are contributing at a high level between meetings. The board members undergo periodic written evaluations. The board does annual assessments (perhaps using the OBE). Purposeful improvement plans are discussed and acted upon. As a result, the business consistently achieves strong results.

Meets Performance

A board that does fairly well in several of the Steps (especially Steps 1 and 4) usually performs at the "meets" level. It has good members, with at least one or two independent experts. It tackles some of the important strategic and policy issues of the business. Tactical discussions are present in meetings but not excessive. Resolutions to real opportunities are sought and realized, but not consistently. Trust is OK. Risk-taking, commitment, and emotional involvement are good. The board works reasonably well together. There are solid contributions by some or most members. Long-term business results are satisfactory, with some years better than others. The business may experience a down year from time to time, primarily due to overall market or economic conditions rather than poor strategic choices.

Weak Performance

The third and lowest level of overall board performance is summed up well in its name: "weak performance." A weak-performing board typically does not have the right members. There is a lack of independent expertise to help the company grow to the next level. Weak-performing boards tend to have a lot of inside members. In some cases there are too many "friends" or "yes people" on the board. Chemistry is low—the board does not work well together. While certain individual members may contribute from time to time, in general, individual board member performance is below average.

Weak-performing boards are usually focused on the wrong issues (tactics versus strategy and policy issues). Members tend to discuss safe topics. They rarely challenge the chair, the CEO, or the executive team. Trust is minimal or uncertain. Weak-performing boards are typically characterized by below-average business results, especially in the long-term measures that count, such as profitability, customer satisfaction, and company value creation.

Moving to a Higher Level

The obvious goal for any board is to move to a higher level of performance. Before a board can do this, it is essential to understand why the board is not performing well. Which of the 5 Steps are contributing to the performance shortfall? Is the chair, the CEO, or the executive team holding back the board's overall performance? Are there things in place that hurt trust? Another key reason could be the board members. Does it have the right expertise represented on the board? Are there specific members who are not contributing? Are there too many inside members? Is the board's purpose unclear? Are there evaluations in place that can help pinpoint opportunities for purposeful improvement?

Regardless, the long-term business results should reflect the caliber of the board members and the caliber and willingness of the executive team to act upon the good advice of the board.

A practical approach to assess overall board performance is to use the Overall Board Evaluation (OBE) diagnostic tool shown in Appendix 7 (in its entirety) and below in Exhibit 11 (first part of the OBE). It takes into account many of the suggestions found in this book. It is also linked to the attributes of good board performance. The OBE parallels the 5 Steps. It makes it easy to assess the board's performance by determining which of the three levels the board is achieving (weak, meets, or peak) for specific criteria related to each of the 5 Steps.

It is a good idea to ask the chair, CEO, and individual board members to do their own OBE assessment. You will have a more complete and accurate picture of the overall board's performance, including what's right and what's wrong with the board. More importantly, the areas of opportunity to improve the board will emerge from the fog so that purposeful improvement can occur.

The OBE should illuminate which of the 5 Steps are strengths and which are opportunities for improvement (weaknesses). It will also uncover specific strengths and weaknesses within each of the 5 Steps. Suggested specific areas to cover among the 5 Steps are shown in the OBE in Appendix 7. They can be adapted to meet your business's specific needs. After strengths and opportunities are identified, they should be prioritized. Again, these will emerge from the comprehensive list as shown in the OBE in Appendix 7 (or your adaptation of it).

After the OBE assessment, you should clearly see where the board is weak, mediocre, or strong. This will form the foundation of how you should purposefully improve the board and move it to a higher level of performance. A plan on how to keep the strengths at a high level and how to improve upon, correct, or remove the weaker areas (opportunities for improvement) should be thought through. Progress against the board improvement plan should be reviewed periodically and shared with the board at least annually.

Recognition Is Motivating

It is good practice for the chair (or CEO) to provide direct feedback to the board at least annually. If the board is performing at a peak level, positive feedback is an ideal way to recognize the impact that the board is having on the business. Use specific examples that reflect the contributions of the board (assuming there are genuine contributions to recognize). This expression of appreciation will serve to fuel continued peak performance by the board. Besides being the right thing to do, there is virtually no out-of-pocket expense to do this. It only costs time and thought. Recognition is one of the most underutilized but most effective motivators, particularly for a group of experts that have many choices of how to spend their time.

Here is a specific recognition tip that the Work Resource Center (WRC is a non-profit board the author was involved with) does very well. WRC has the entire executive team sign a card with personalized and specific comments of thanks. The personalized card is sent to each board member during the year-end holidays. From personal experience of being on the receiving end, it has tangible impact and is motivating.

Example of an OBE

Below is the Right Team (Step 1) part of the OBE. The OBE follows the 5 Steps. The complete OBE is included in Appendix 7 and includes all 5 Steps. Each Step is broken down into sub-questions that are used to specifically diagnose where the board is performing well and where it is not performing well. Modify the OBE example to suit your specific board and business needs. For example, if your business has an advisory board, you will want to leave out questions that are not relevant.

Exhibit 11. The Overall Board Evaluation (OBE):

Right Team: Step 1

Evaluation Criteria (Step 1)	Weak	Meets	Peak
➤ Ethics			
➤ Trust			
➤ Confidentiality			
➤ Commitment			
➤ Consistently High Output			
➤ Preparation			
➤ Participation			
➤ Number of Members			
➤ Outside: Inside Ratio (Independence)			
➤ Board Leadership			
➤ Balanced Team			
➤ Builds Upon Strengths			
➤ Compliments Weaknesses			
➤ Quality of Expertise			
➤ Variety of Expertise			
➤ Works Well Together (fit)			
➤ Judgment of Board			
➤ Business Acumen of Board			
➤ Listening Ability of Board			
➤ Expression of Own POV			
➤ Invention/Creativity			
➤ Sensitivity to Family Issues			
➤ Sensitivity to High Growth			
➤ Organized Recruiting Effort			
➤ Board Competency Matrix			
➤ Member Role Description			
➤ Reference Checking			
➤ Ongoing Scouting			
➤ **Overall: Step 1**			

Benchmark Best Practices

One approach to help a board improve is to benchmark against other good boards. This can be done informally or formally. Obtaining information on how other companies successfully run their boards can lead to tangible ideas that work. If you approach another company's board to benchmark, realize that it is common practice to reciprocate.

19. How to Evaluate and Improve CEO Effectiveness

"The secret of success is to do the common things uncommonly well."

—John D. Rockefeller, Jr., son of history's first recorded billionaire, who spent his life giving away the vast fortune earned by his father

19. How to Evaluate and Improve CEO Effectiveness

Accountability Improves Performance

The CEO is usually the chair (leader) of the board in small to midsize closely held companies. As such, an important part of Step 5 *(Right Evaluation)* is to assess the CEO's performance and then develop improvement plans. The positive tension that exists between the board and the CEO is very beneficial as long as there is some accountability. Ideally, the CEO should view the board as his or her boss, even if the CEO owns the company or it is an advisory board. (Recall that technically, an advisory board has no legal power over the CEO.)

CEO accountability to the board is the essence of board independence, which should contribute to higher performance. In small to midsize closely held businesses, from a practical matter, it is difficult to dismiss an owner if he or she is not performing well. Even though that may be the situation, every CEO should be willing to undergo a board evaluation of his or her performance. At least the CEO will have the benefit of receiving valuable feedback. Only he or she can decide what to do with it. Hopefully, the CEO will take the evaluation to heart and use it as an opportunity to improve. If not, over time, good board members may lose interest as they may feel they are wasting their time. Even more concerning is the likely impact on the business. If the leader is unwilling to improve, business results will probably suffer.

Use Established, Objective Criteria

Reviews should be based upon established, objective criteria. Select a few (three to five should be ample) of the most important business results (the scorecard). Profitability, return on assets, customer satisfaction, return on investment, revenue growth, enterprise value (creation), and cash flow are among the more important results to consider. These measures should be taken from the strategic plan. Beyond concrete business measures, the behaviors and responsibilities identified in Chapter 5 *(How the CEO Can Maximize Board Effectiveness)* are worth considering for evaluation.

Use a Written Evaluation Form

Similar to the board member and OBE evaluation processes, it is best to do CEO evaluations in writing. There is an example of an easy-to-use CEO evaluation form in Exhibit 12 below, and in Appendix 8. Like the board member and OBE forms, the CEO is rated on a scale from one (poor/weak) to ten (excellent/peak) for each evaluation criteria. The suggested criteria are consistent with the characteristics of an effective CEO (some of which were discussed in Chapter 5).

The evaluation is straightforward. A check mark is placed in the column appropriate for the CEO's performance. As you can see in Exhibit 12 below, the first three evaluation criteria (1, 2, and 3) are based on concrete long-term measures that should be taken directly from the strategic plan. You should use the two or three metrics that are most relevant for your business. Criteria 4 and 5 reflect the importance of having a good plan and focusing on that plan. The remaining categories (criteria 7 through 15) are important attributes of an effective CEO. These fifteen criteria shown in Exhibit 12 are suggestions. Modify them, add or subtract criteria, as appropriate for your business needs.

On the back of the CEO evaluation form, there is space for written comments that cannot be easily captured in the checklist format. These should be specific and related to the goals and expected behaviors noted above.

Exhibit 12. CEO Evaluation Criteria

Peak-Performance, Inc.
CEO Evaluation

CEO's Name:

Date of Evaluation:

Evaluation Period (from, to):

Board Evaluator's Name (and signature):

Please rate the CEO on each of the evaluation criteria below. This evaluation is intended to provide the CEO with feedback and a point of discussion so that the CEO can continue to improve. Responses will be shared in a consensus report. Your individual responses will be kept confidential.

Evaluation Criteria	Weak (Poor)			Meets (Satisfactory)				Peak (Excellent)		
	1	2	3	4	5	6	7	8	9	10
1. Revenue Results										
2. Profit Results										
3. Enterprise Value Results										
4. Strategic Plan (right plan)										
5. Focuses on Strategy/Policy										
6. Leadership										
7. Quality of Executive Team										
8. Teamwork										
9. Open Communication/Trust										
10. Listening										
11. Integrity										
12. Rigor and Discipline										
13. Lives by Values/Culture										
14. Willingness to Improve/Learn										
15. Overall Effectiveness										

Mutual Evaluations Improve Accuracy

Similar to the board mutual evaluation process, it is suggested that the CEO and each board member fill out the CEO Evaluation Form. This should be done autonomously. Having both perspectives will likely improve accuracy.

Provide Consensus Feedback

CEO performance should be evaluated on a yearly basis using the same criteria (assuming the criteria are still relevant). After the evaluations are independently analyzed and complete, the board should meet and come to a consensus evaluation. Specifically, a consensus evaluation is a compilation that reflects the input of all outside board members. The consensus evaluation will likely identify strengths and areas to improve. It should be compared to the CEO's self-evaluation. Any gross misperceptions should be identified for discussion.

The evaluation should be shared directly with the CEO. The discussion should recognize and encourage continuation of strengths. It should also focus on opportunities to improve. Tangible next steps should be identified with input from both the board and the CEO.

Other Methods of CEO Evaluation

There are many leadership evaluation approaches and tools, such as a 360-degree review, among internal and external customers, and evaluation forms and processes created by independent consultants or organization development companies. One example is the Leadership Practices Inventory (LPI), a quantitative performance assessment tool published by Jossey Bass. The Web site to obtain information on the LPI is: www.the*leadershipchallenge.com*.

The LPI was developed by Jim Kouzes and Barry Possner. The premise behind the LPI is that leadership can be learned and improved. The LPI categorizes leadership performance into "practices" that were identified among extraordinary leaders. Specifically, they found that exceptional leaders challenge, inspire, enable, model, and encourage.

The LPI is just one example of the many tools available to assess and improve CEO performance. The important point is to consistently do CEO evaluations, whether you use an adaptation of the one included in this book, the LPI, or some other tool.

Another corporate-wide evaluation tool that has become popular is the Balanced Scorecard. If used properly, it is an effective performance goal and evaluation tool. The Balanced Scorecard does a good job of aligning performance metrics throughout the organization.

Here is a word of caution when using the Balanced Scorecard evaluation approach. Many companies that implement a Balanced Scorecard tend to use too many metrics to evaluate performance. Doing this can cause a dilution in focus. The author recommends focusing on fewer, more important evaluation metrics or criteria versus having a laundry list of every imaginable metric of performance. Net, the Balanced Scorecard is an excellent tool if used in a "balanced" way.

SPECIAL BOARD CONSIDERATIONS

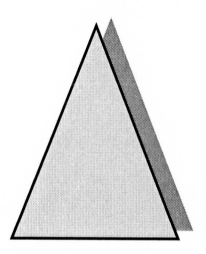

This section covers special board considerations. The two most prevalent in small to midsize private companies are family and start-up (entrepreneurial) companies. While the board effectiveness principles already discussed in this book apply to these two situations, there are additional complications. The good news is that a few tips can help overcome unique complexities of these two "special" types of businesses.

The first chapter covers intergenerational dysfunction and other issues that can crop up in family businesses. The next chapter addresses start-up businesses, particularly the difficult transitions that can occur due to hyper-growth. There is a chapter that provides considerations and tips for serving on other boards. The last chapter covers board considerations for Sarbanes-Oxley, a recent law that mostly affects public companies but can affect certain private companies.

20. Family Board Matters

"Happiness is having a large, loving, caring, close-knit family in another city."

—George Burns, one of America's most beloved entertainers and comedians

20. Family Board Matters

Family Businesses Need Independent Boards

Small to midsize family businesses need independent boards just as much as, if not more than, non-family businesses due to unique complexities they face. Role conflict among family members, intergenerational dynamics, and misalignment of goals with and within the family and business can create complications. To put the challenges of family businesses into perspective, consider the fact that only about one out of three family businesses successfully transitions to the second generation.

Having an independent board can reduce the internal friction or emotional issues among family members who have a stake in the business. Another point to consider is that some family businesses lack professional management. A good independent board can be very helpful in this situation.

A Caveat: Sensitivity to Family Issues

All of the 5 Steps apply to family business boards. The principles for identifying and recruiting family business board experts (Step 1) are the same as any other business. However, there is a caveat. Family businesses need to find board members who will be *sensitive* to family issues. Family business board members must be able to understand and work with family members who may not see things from a purely "what's right for the business" perspective. Family business board members should also have an appreciation for and understanding that dysfunctional family relationships can occur and should be managed.

Sometimes, the agendas of the family and the business do not align. This can cause significant problems. A crucial role the board can play is to ensure that the agendas of the family and the business are aligned. If there are different opinions as to which path to pursue, someone needs to determine, should the business or the family come first? Who makes the call? How does management best navigate through these conflicts? The board is in a unique position to help settle differences between the family and the business.

Transfer of power from one generation to another can be very sticky in family businesses. In some situations, the older generation may not be willing to let go of the reins. In other cases, the son(s) or daughter(s) may not be prepared or capable of taking the reins.

Snafus also occur with the transfer of stock to other generations or family members. For example, in the interest of "fairness," sometimes the business ownership (including voting rights) is dispersed evenly among the children or grandchildren. This often occurs even though some of the siblings are not involved in the business while others are. It also occurs where family members do not have business acumen. While this may seem to be the "fair" thing to do, it can seriously hinder the long-term success of the business. The problem is that no one has a crystal ball to know if the business will be in jeopardy because future generations do not see eye-to-eye.

The fact is that family businesses are often adversely affected when an ownership plan is not thought through from both perspectives; what is right for the family and what is right for the business. Alternative approaches should be strongly considered prior to the transfer of stock to all family members. A good board can help. There may be more prudent ways to compensate family members fairly without dividing up the voting power of the company among disparate owners.

Shown below in Exhibit 13 is a short list of the many potential issues that can emerge in a family business. This list dimensionalizes the added complexities and reinforces the need for an independent board for a family business.

Exhibit 13. Potential Family Business Issues

❖ **Overall Board Governance**
- ➤ What type of board is best for the family business? (See Chapter 9, *Establish the Right Board for Your Business Needs.*)
- ➤ Should family members be on the board? If so, why those particular members?
- ➤ Should family members be involved in selecting the board?
- ➤ What should the board's purpose be as it relates to the business and the family? (See Chapter 10, *How to Develop a Useful Board Constitution.*)
- ➤ Whom should the board report to? Why?
- ➤ What does a next-generation family member do if he or she inherits a board that is not very effective? (See Chapter 18, *How to Evaluate and Improve Board Effectiveness.*)
- ➤ What should the board do if the family members do not respect the board?

❖ **Family Involvement in the Business**
- ➤ Who should be involved in the business among the family members, spouses, relatives, etc.? (See Chapter 7, *Keys to Identifying Great Board Members.*)
- ➤ What are the criteria to qualify for working in the family business?
- ➤ Should the next CEO be a family member? Why or why not?
- ➤ Should any family members attend board meetings? If so, who and when?
- ➤ How does the business handle or manage difficult family members (or sometimes worse, difficult spouses)?

❖ **Compensation**
- ➤ What represents "fair compensation" when there are multiple family members doing different jobs within the company? (See Chapter 11, *Tips on Board Compensation.*)

> ➢ How should dividends be handled? Do the business or the family needs come first? What happens when there are different financial needs among family members?

❖ **Performance Evaluation**
> ➢ How do the family and/or board evaluate the performance of the CEO? (See Chapter 19, *How to Evaluate and Improve CEO Effectiveness.*)
> ➢ What happens if the CEO is not performing well?
> ➢ Should the company evaluate family members differently than professional mangers? Why or why not?

❖ **Ownership Transfer**
> ➢ How does the board ensure a smooth transition if there is a transfer of ownership from one generation to the next?
> ➢ Is there a buy-sell agreement (hopefully)?
> ➢ How does the buy-sell agreement deal with issues such as liquidity, protecting company cash or future ownership?
> ➢ Should there be different classes of stock (e.g. voting, non-voting)?
> ➢ How does the family obtain buy-in to different classes of stock?
> ➢ What happens if the older generation will not let go of the reins?
> ➢ What happens if the younger generation is not ready to take the reins (how does the board know if they are ready or not)?
> ➢ If there is a sale from one generation to another, how does everyone get comfortable with the valuation of the business?
> ➢ How does the company repurchase shares from family members that are not involved in the business?
> ➢ How does the company assure financial security for the older generation, post-exit?
> ➢ What happens to family ownership when there are events other than death such as health problems or hardship cases?

> ➤ How should matters like prenuptial agreements and divorce be handled that present potential risks to the family and business?

❖ **Communication**
> ➤ What is the best communication process between the family and the business?
> ➤ Who manages the communication flow between family members and the company?
> ➤ What role does the board play with respect to communicating directly with the family?
> ➤ What information should be shared (the same information to all family members or not, why or why not)?

Jump-Start Your Family Board

The above list (Exhibit 13) shows why it is a good idea to recruit at least one board member who has successful experience in serving on family business boards. This person can "jump-start" the board so that it proactively addresses the tough issues listed in Exhibit 13 (and others) that are unique to family businesses and that many family businesses will likely face.

Avoid the Temptation

Oftentimes, family members who are owners want to be on the board. After all, they have a financial stake and consequently are interested in the success of the enterprise. *Be careful!* It is a big mistake to clutter a board with family members who are owners. Ideally, the only "insiders" (non-independent board members) in a small to midsize family business who should be considered for board membership are the CEO, COO, or CFO (similar to non-family small business boards) *and* the key next generation family member(s). The new successor should join the board shortly before a leadership transition occurs, and not too soon. Board members and participation is covered in Chapter 10 *(How to Develop a Useful Board Constitution)* as part of the board constitution.

Establish a Family Forum

One way to help reduce pressure to have many family members on the board is to establish a separate Family Forum that looks after the needs of the family. It can serve as a forum for communicating and resolving issues that relate to the business. Just as important, it will help to separate business policy and strategy from family policy and agendas, which are sometimes not aligned.

21. The Entrepreneur's Board: A Different Breed

"Restlessness is discontent, and discontent is the first necessity of progress."

—Thomas Alva Edison, with little formal schooling, illuminated the path of progress through his inventions. He is credited with 1,093 patents in telegraphy, phonography, electric lighting, photography, and motion pictures, among others.

21. The Entrepreneur's Board: A Different Breed

Jump-Start Your Start-Up

Entrepreneurs typically do not start with a board, yet they can benefit the most in the early years. Plato said: "The beginning is the most important part of the work." Plato was right when it comes to starting a business. There are so many pitfalls. Everything appears to be moving at hyper-speed. Entrepreneurial companies experience a high failure rate. Having an appropriate independent board can jump-start the business. It can increase the chances for success.

Start Small

Every great company started out with a founder (or a few people) with a vision. The early stages of a business need a lot of nurturing, guidance, and help. Entrepreneurs can really benefit from "experts" who have gone through a start-up. Preferably, these start-up "experts" should be open-minded, and calculated risk takers (versus inflexible and risk-averse). They should have experience with the early stages of a start-up company. Just as important, they must be able to impose some discipline on the founder(s). These are rare but invaluable board members. They are worth their weight in gold.

To get things underway, start with two or three independent members. As mentioned above, at least one board member should have experienced entrepreneurial success. For a second member, consider an expert who can help with the most critical business need. For example, if you have a large marketing challenge, recruit a board member who knows that world well (especially if this area is not your forté). The third expert should balance out the board team. They should bring unique expertise linked to the greatest need to ensure success. Perhaps they have expertise in gaining customers from within the company's industry or market. Having knowledge of the sales process and a strong customer network can make a big difference during a company's early stages.

Having just a few board members initially will provide easier communication and "hands-on intimacy." This closeness is very important in the volatile, infant phase of a new business.

Another important prerequisite for the initial two or three independent board members of high-growth, start-up companies is *flexibility*. The initial members must be willing to adapt. They should be reasonably responsive to the dynamic needs of the entrepreneur(s). Just as important though, the board must be able to have enough influence to guide the entrepreneur(s).

Don't Think Big

A common mistake made among start-up boards is to recruit executives from big businesses. While large company candidates may have excellent overall business credentials, they may not understand the unique dynamics and hands-on nature of a start-up operation. Save the qualified large company board candidates for when the business makes a transition from a start-up to a more mature, professionally run business. One exception to this guideline is if the start-up has large companies as its potential customers. In this case, recruiting a board member with a strong network into potential customers can be very advantageous.

Cash Is King and Queen

It is important for any new business to become cash flow positive as soon as possible. After all, cash is the lifeblood of any business. Every entrepreneur needs help in cutting the cash umbilical cord. There is a different mentality in small versus large businesses. The entrepreneur must spend within cash constraints versus spending to a budget.

An important oversight responsibility of the board in the early stages of a business is to help ensure that the company has adequate cash to grow. Board members can provide critical insights into what financial institutions, such as banks, VCs, angel investors, leasing companies, and other potential sources of cash, are looking for. A good business plan is one thing, but there are many other nuances. Having an experienced veteran on your side can really help you navigate through the cash crunch.

Board members can also open doors to these cash kings and queens. That benefit alone can sometimes assure the initial survival and ultimate success of a company.

Here is a tip to conserve cash as it relates to boards. Consider initially structuring board compensation with long-term incentives such as stock options, SARs, phantom stock, and the like, versus a retainer or meeting fees. This will help the company manage precious cash. It will also reward board members based upon the ultimate success of the company. As the company grows, it can migrate to a combination of meeting and retainer fees, and long-term rewards, as appropriate.

Add Members Before Transitions

After the business is up and running, the company should add new board members *before* critical needs arise or major transitions occur. This is an adaptation of Step 1. The Board Search Description in Appendix 1 is a good example of how to infuse the appropriate expertise before it is needed. For example, Peak-Performance, Inc. will need IPO, acquisitions, and Sarbanes-Oxley expertise. Thus, it is seeking to recruit the right financial board expert *before* the need arises.

It is much better to inject the right expertise into the company through the board than to try to learn a difficult and potentially costly lesson. The problem is that this notion goes against the grain of most entrepreneurs. They often believe that they can figure out almost anything on their own. This "can do" attitude and unbridled tenacity are a few of the reasons entrepreneurs often beat the odds.

Make no mistake, though. If you have ever done an IPO or bought a company, you know that these are very sophisticated and involved games. So why increase the chances for failure? An IPO or an acquisition is something with which the founder usually has very little experience. If you are going to be in the IPO or acquisitions game, consider recruiting an expert who has prior experience with these complex transactions.

The principle of bringing specific expertise before it is needed applies to other transitions of high-growth, entrepreneurial companies as well. For example, most high-growth companies go though a transition when professional management becomes essential.

The Professional Management Transition

Every company goes through transitions. Fast-growing, entrepreneurial companies just go through them quicker. As such, growing pains can be more hurtful. The right board expertise can minimize this pain. It can reduce costly mistakes. One common and often difficult transition is when professional management is needed to grow the company to the next level.

The entrepreneur's board must be sensitive to this and other transitions. It should help the founder successfully migrate through these experiences where a lot of companies falter. A great board will help an entrepreneur to "give up the reins" yet stay involved in the company, focusing on his or her particular competencies.

One special company stands out as a role model of how to make a smooth transition into a professionally managed company. eBay is a true entrepreneurial success story. The founder, Pierre Omidyar, started the business by listening to his girlfriend, who was frustrated. She had difficulty in finding local trading partners for her Pez collection. Yes, the idea for a global garage sale where everyone has access to the same information was brilliant. There was an almost insatiable need for an efficient auction process that matched the right buyers and sellers. However, the idea was only part of Pierre's genius. One could argue that the real breakthrough was the realization that the company grew beyond his competencies. Pierre understood that eBay would need professional management to reach the next level of success. To that end, Meg Whitman and other professional managers were recruited to the team at the right time. Very few entrepreneurial companies have made this transition as well as eBay. An independent board can help those of us who are not as wise as Pierre Omidyar.

The Succession Plan/Exit Transition

Some entrepreneurs are guilty of believing that "their" company will be with them forever. Many do not consider a succession or exit plan unless forced to do so. An independent board can be instrumental in ensuring a smooth exit or transition to new leadership, when appropriate.

22. Tips for Serving on Other Boards

"The best moments usually occur when a person's mind is stretched to its limit in a voluntary effort to accomplish something difficult and worthwhile."

—Mihaly Csikszentmihalyi, author, professor and former chairman of the Department of Psychology at the University of Chicago

22. Tips For Serving On Other Boards

Serving on a Board Is a Responsibility

Sometimes, successful people accept a position to serve on a business board for the wrong reason. They think of the position as a reward for good deeds done elsewhere. This is not a good reason to join a board. If you are fortunate enough to be offered a board seat in a small to midsize business (or any business), you should view it as a *responsibility*. After all, the company is entrusting its future in your hands. If a potential board member treats the position as a trophy, they do not deserve to be on the board.

Serving on Other Boards Can Be Rewarding

Serving on another board can help you run your own board and business more effectively. The knowledge you capture from the business challenges that you will be exposed to and the wisdom you will obtain from other board members (experts) almost guarantees this. Every board meeting has something to teach, as does every board member. Every CEO has his or her own approaches too. If you are open-minded, observe and listen, you will learn numerous things to take back to your own board and company. Some learning will be positive—what to reapply to your company. Other learning will be mistakes—what to avoid in your company. Both are valuable.

Another benefit to serving on other boards is the gratitude and pride that come from helping others. It is very rewarding to see people learn, grow, and succeed.

The potential benefits of serving on other boards continue to accrue. Your network will expand and you might even find friendship among the other board members. After all, you will be spending intense idea-sharing, problem solving, and strategic thinking time together over a period of years.

Evaluate Yourself Before You Accept

If you are fortunate enough to be asked to serve on a board, you should conduct a thorough personal evaluation before you accept. Below is a list of questions you may want to ask yourself before proceeding:

➤ Do you trust the CEO, executive team, and other board members?

➤ Do you believe in the company's plan?

➤ If you answer no to either of these two questions on trust or belief, *do not join.*

➤ Is the chemistry good? You will be spending a lot of time together. You want to make sure you can get along with the CEO, executive team, and other board members.

➤ Are you prepared to make the commitment and accept the responsibility? Serving on an outside board is a demanding part-time job. It can be stressful. You will be partially responsible for the company's future successes or failures. Do you want to engage in the turmoil? If not, then it is better to shy away from the responsibility.

➤ Do you have the right expertise that the company desires? Related questions that should be asked are: Can you contribute in a meaningful way... can you succeed? Ask yourself, "Why have they asked me to serve on their board?" Be honest. If it is just for your name or connections, you may become disillusioned over time. If they think you have a skill or expertise that you do not possess, that is a problem. It is flattering to be asked. However, do not partake if you do not have the skills or competencies that are required.

➤ Can you learn from management and the other board members? This is important to understand. A main reason for participating on other boards is to learn and grow.

➤ Are they paying me fairly? As mentioned in Chapter 11 *(Tips on Board Compensation),* compensation should not be the primary reason for joining a board. Therefore, you may still agree to join another board if the compensation is lower than norms. However, there should be other benefits that you can realize that will offset low compensation.

Conduct Due Diligence

If you decide that you can and want to help and there is initial trust and belief in the business, don't immediately say "yes." Conduct due diligence so you are informed as to what you are getting into. How much due diligence effort you want to put forth depends on your own risk profile. It also depends on your perception of how risky the board position is versus what the board position can offer you. There is a range of due diligence questions you can ask. Listed below are a few of the important questions to think about asking before you decide to join another board:

➤ How thorough has the company been with you? Be careful if the company only does a cursory or superficial job in qualifying you. You may want to ask what the company did to qualify or evaluate your credentials. The exception is if there is prior knowledge of your qualifications.

➤ How good is the board chemistry? You want a board with high trust where ideas and information flow freely and the CEO rewards a healthy give-and-take (dissension is OK). You do not want a "yes" board where board members conform to and "obey" the CEO.

➤ How well does the board perform in each of the 5 Steps?

➤ How would the Overall Board Evaluation (OBE, covered in Chapter 18, *How to Evaluate and Improve Board Effectiveness*) come out? Would it be a Peak, Meets, or Weak performer? If a "Weak" or "Meets" performer, can it evolve into a peak-performing board and company? If the company conducts written board evaluations, you may want to see recent examples.

➤ Is there a board constitution and code of ethics? Are they well thought out and appropriate? Are the roles clear?

➤ Does the company have D&O insurance? Probe to understand what is covered and what is not covered. (See Chapter 12, *Ways to Protect Board Members.*) If it is a public company or a business that is in a high-risk situation, you may want to see the actual

D&O insurance policy. Here is a tip: Just because a company has an appropriate D&O insurance policy in place, it does not mean that you should join the board. If board members are likely to be sued, you probably do not want to be involved, even with D&O insurance. The world has changed, post-Enron. Ask any board member who has been through a legal suit. Even if there is no fault and appropriate insurance is in place, the legal process can be very time-consuming and draining. Sometimes a company is sued because there is insurance. Lawyers sometimes go after deep pockets (i.e. insurance), regardless of fault.

➤ Ask if the company has ever been sued, how many times it has been sued, and if there have been any judgments against it. In some situations, you may want a litigation search done. A large number of lawsuits and/or several judgments should be seen as a red flag.

➤ How good are the executive team and the other board members? How does the CEO stack up against the criteria in Chapter 5 (*How the CEO Can Maximize Board Effectiveness*)? Look and determine what the other board members are like. How do they stack up against the success criteria set forth in Chapter 6 (*What Makes Great Board Members?*)? Consider doing reference checking on the company, its management, and its board. You may want to make time to interview selected executives and/or board members. Find out if your expectations match their views on the company.

➤ Does the company have a written strategic plan? If so, you may want to see the actual plan or a summary of the strategic plan. Are the opportunities and risks realistic, reasonable, and acceptable? Of note, it is OK to join a board without a written strategic plan. A new board can serve as a catalyst to create the plan. However, it may take more time to evaluate the risks and opportunities of joining a board.

➤ Ask to review historical and current financial information. You want to fully grasp the financial health and risks of the company and evaluate its future prospects for success.

➤ Carefully look at and understand the balance sheet. Is the company highly leveraged and are there bankruptcy risks or uncorrectable cash flow concerns? Many serious board liability problems stem from poor financial balance sheets. You want to avoid highly leveraged situations, unless you can accept the potential consequences and you deem the benefits will outweigh the hardships of serving on the board.

➢ Are the key financial and legal advisors competent? Consider speaking with the company's legal counsel and accounting firm.

➢ How solid is the customer base? Getting in touch (with management's approval) with key customers may provide good insights into the company and aid in your decision.

➢ In conclusion, you want to have a reasonable idea of what you are getting into before you make a commitment. It is much better to ask up front than to be disappointed later on. Besides, this qualification process will help orient you to the business if you do decide to join the board.

Need a Trial Run?

Still undecided? You probably should not join if the above questions are answered properly and the answers are acceptable. However, there is another option to explore which can get at a lot of the above questions in one meeting. Specifically, ask the chair (or CEO) if you can observe a board meeting without making a firm commitment. This "trial run" will enable you to see the inner workings of the board and can be invaluable in assessing if the board is right for you and vice-versa.

Self-Check

If you do accept the board position, use the ideas from this book and your own experiences to help you be a peak-performing board member. Conduct a Self-Check (see Exhibit 14 below). It categorizes your performance by the three levels: "Weak," "Meets," and "Peak." (See Chapter 18.)

This self-diagnostic tool is related to Step 5 *(Right Improvement)*. It mainly covers Steps 3 and 4. That's because the Right Team (Step 1) and Right Framework (Step 2) are already in place.

The Self-Check is an easy way to evaluate your performance on other boards. It will determine where you are performing well. It will also expose areas where you can improve. Fill it out before deciding to join a board and periodically after joining a board. Analyze your results. Determine areas of strength (so that you can build upon or maintain them) and develop an action plan for the areas that you can improve.

Exhibit 14. Board Performance Self-Check

Board Member Self-Check
Board Meeting Date(s): _____

Category	Weak	Meets	Peak	NA
➢ Preparation				
➢ Participation				
➢ Offered Useful Advice				
➢ Focused on Strategy/Policy				
➢ Avoided Tactical Discussions				
➢ Helped Invent				
➢ Listened Well				
➢ Expressed Own POV				
➢ Was a Team Player				
➢ Challenged the Status Quo				
➢ Helped Identify Risks				
➢ Offered Creative Solutions				
➢ Helped Network				
➢ Instilled Accountability				
➢ Helped with Succession/Exit				
➢ Overall Evaluation				

---

23. Sarbanes-Oxley Considerations

"To reform a man you must begin with his grandmother."

—Victor Marie Hugo, a novelist, poet, and dramatist, considered among the most important French Romantic writers

23. Sarbanes-Oxley Considerations

A recent law that has had broad impact on public companies and limited impact (in most cases) on private companies is Sarbanes-Oxley. Of note, if Sarbanes-Oxley is not relevant to your business, you may want to skip this chapter.

President George W. Bush signed into law the Sarbanes-Oxley Act in July 2002. This law of sweeping changes created an oversight board to "police" the accounting industry. It also toughened penalties against executives who commit corporate fraud and increased the Securities and Exchange Commission (SEC) budget for compliance auditors and investigators. The law had a secondary objective to restore investor confidence in the U.S. stock markets.

Sarbanes-Oxley represents one of the biggest changes in corporate governance reform since laws were created after the Great Depression, back in the early-to-mid-1930s. Sarbanes-Oxley was drafted in response to corporate governance and accounting improprieties at Enron, Tyco, WorldCom, and other large, publicly traded companies. These bad apples shook the public's confidence in corporate America.

A stated objective of Sarbanes-Oxley is *"To protect investors by improving the accuracy and reliability of corporate disclosures made pursuant to the securities laws, and for other purposes."* It has truly affected public company boards.

Sarbanes-Oxley can be complicated. As such, it is subject to misunderstandings. Further, compliance with Sarbanes-Oxley can be costly, especially for public companies. So why bother with Sarbanes-Oxley if you are involved with a private company? Although Sarbanes-Oxley does not directly affect corporate governance and financial reporting practices of private companies in the same broad-scale manner that it affects public companies, for the most part, private companies could benefit from voluntarily adopting improved governance and financial reporting practices. Additionally, there are explicit situations where certain private companies may be directly affected by Sarbanes-Oxley. These situations will be revealed below. Lastly, over time, judgmentally Sarbanes-Oxley will likely have more influence over private company governance as stakeholders seek better safeguards over their investments.

An entire book could be written on Sarbanes-Oxley, its provisions, and associated compliance requirements. As such, it is recommended that appropriate experts help public and private companies with Sarbanes-Oxley compliance requirements.

To orient you to Sarbanes-Oxley, below are highlights as they relate to directors of *public* companies. These highlights are followed by specific Sarbanes-Oxley considerations for private company boards.

> **Corporate Responsibility/Board Independence** — Overall, there is an increase in CEO, CFO, and board member accountability and responsibility with the advent of Sarbanes-Oxley. Power has shifted to public company boards from executive management. This means greater board member responsibilities and subsequently, potential liabilities.

> **Board Independence** — Sarbanes-Oxley has resulted in the SEC establishing new requirements regarding board composition, structure, and process, and other corporate governance matters. These new standards address the definition of director independence, the composition and responsibilities of the audit committee, the requirement for an audit committee charter, and the requirement for independent directors and independent committees. The requirement for independent directors and independent committees includes provisions that: a majority of board members be independent; executive sessions of independent directors are held; and independent oversight of executive compensation and director nominations exist.

Independent Audit Committee — As mentioned, Sarbanes-Oxley requires an independent audit committee. That committee has responsibility to select and oversee the company's independent accountant; procedures for handling complaints regarding the company's accounting practices; the authority of the audit committee to engage advisors; and funding for the independent auditor and any outside advisors engaged by the audit committee. Additionally, Sections 406 and 407 of Sarbanes-Oxley require public companies to disclose if they have an "audit committee financial expert." Sarbanes-Oxley's independent audit committee requirements will be covered in more detail towards the end of this chapter.

Blackout Period — Section 306(a) prohibits any director or executive officer of an issuer of any equity security from directly or indirectly purchasing, selling, or otherwise acquiring or transferring any equity security of the issuer during a pension plan blackout period that temporarily prevents plan participants or beneficiaries from engaging in equity securities transactions through their plan accounts, if the director or executive officer acquired the equity security in connection with his or her service or employment as a director or executive officer. In addition, the rules specify the content and timing of the notice that companies must provide to their directors and executive officers and to the SEC about a blackout period.

➤ **Enhanced Financial Disclosures**—As a result of Sarbanes-Oxley, the CEO and CFO have more responsibility and accountability to certify the completeness and accuracy of financial statements, disclosure controls and procedures, and internal controls to the SEC. Sarbanes-Oxley requires a public company's principal executive and financial officers each to certify the financial and other information contained in the company's quarterly and annual reports. Public company directors have oversight responsibility in these areas.

Off-Balance Sheet Disclosures — As a result of Sarbanes-Oxley, the board must be more involved in the review of Management's Discussion and Analysis disclosure ("MD&A"). Sarbanes-Oxley requires disclosure of off-balance sheet arrangements. It specifically requires management to provide an explanation of its off-balance sheet arrangements in a separately captioned subsection of the MD&A section of a company's disclosure documents. It also requires companies (other than small businesses) to provide an overview of certain known contractual obligations.

Internal Controls — Public company board members need to be aware of internal control systems and procedures. Section 404 of Sarbanes-Oxley requires a company's management to present an internal control report in the company's annual report containing: (1) a statement of the responsibility of management for establishing and maintaining an adequate internal control structure and procedures for financial reporting; and (2) an assessment, as of the end of the company's most recent fiscal year, of the effectiveness of the company's internal control structure and procedures for financial reporting. Section 404 also requires the company's registered public accounting firm to attest to, and report on, management's assessment.

Document Retention — Public company board members should be aware that Sarbanes-Oxley requires a document retention policy. Sarbanes-Oxley states that companies and their boards cannot falsify or cover up documents that impede, obstruct, or influence a federal investigation. If found guilty, there are fines and/or prison term penalties for knowingly altering, destroying, concealing, or falsifying any record, document, or tangible object with intent to impede, obstruct, or influence the investigation or administration of any matter within the jurisdiction of any department or agency of the U.S. of any bankruptcy case.

Additionally, as a result of Sarbanes-Oxley, the SEC has new rules requiring accounting firms to retain certain records relevant to their audits and reviews of company financial statements. Records to be retained include an accounting firm's work papers and certain other documents that contain conclusions, opinions, analyses, or financial data related to the audit or review.

Ethical Behavior Guidelines—Sarbanes-Oxley requires the company to disclose whether it has adopted a code of ethics for it senior financial officers. In essence, it necessitates establishing a code of conduct and ethics, having proper disclosures, preventing compensation abuses, and limiting fraud. It prohibits officers and directors and persons acting under the direction of an officer or director, from taking any action to fraudulently influence, coerce, manipulate, or mislead the auditor of a company's financial statements for the purpose of rendering the financial statements materially misleading. There are also conflict of interest requirements and disclosures related to research analysts, brokers, investment bankers, and the company.

➤ **Auditor Independence** — Sarbanes-Oxley changes the role of the auditor. It prohibits an auditor from performing specified non-audit services at the same time as audit work is done. Specifically, the company's auditor can no longer conduct other business that could create a conflict of interest. Sarbanes-Oxley also requires that auditors report directly to the audit committee and that appropriate accounting policies and practices are used in the audit.

➤ **Fraud, Crime, and Penalties**—As a result of Sarbanes-Oxley, fraud and criminal abuses are more defined and have harsher penalties. Below are highlights of some of these changes.

Corporate Fraud Accountability — Sarbanes-Oxley imposes criminal penalties for knowingly destroying, altering, concealing of falsifying records with intent to obstruct or influence either a federal investigation or a matter in bankruptcy and for failure of an auditor to maintain, for a five-year period, all audit or review work papers.

Whistleblower Provision — Sarbanes-Oxley also provides a whistleblower provision. Specifically, companies must provide company employees and their accountants the right and means to anonymously notify federal regulators or corporate audit committees of any potential wrongdoing within their company. This provision prohibits an employer from taking certain actions against employees who lawfully disclose employer information to, among others, parties in a judicial proceeding involving a fraud claim. If a company takes action against a "whistleblower," and is found guilty, there are fines and/or prison term penalties that can occur. Whistleblowers may also be granted a remedy of special damages and attorney's fees.

White Collar Crime Penalty Enhancements — Sarbanes-Oxley establishes criminal liability for failure of corporate officers to certify financial reports. Any attempt to commit or conspire to commit an offense under a white-collar crime or consumer protection law is punishable to the extent of the underlying crime. Penalties are increased for mail or wire fraud. Penalties are also increased for ERISA violations. There is even a corporate fraud hotline that was installed by the FBI where callers can call in anonymously (888-622-0117). In addition to the phone number, the FBI has special agents with accounting skills to ferret out corporate fraud.

Sarbanes-Oxley Private Company Considerations

Even though Sarbanes-Oxley was created primarily for public companies and their boards of directors, there has and will likely continue to be a cascading effect onto private companies and their boards (statuary, not advisory boards). Below are specific provisions of Sarbanes-Oxley that currently directly apply to private companies as well as public companies. It is recommended that private companies establish or amend applicable retirement plan, employment, and document retention policies and procedures in order to incorporate these aspects of Sarbanes-Oxley.

➢ **Whistleblower Provision** — As with public companies, private companies need to provide informants the right and means to anonymously notify federal regulators or corporate audit committees (if any) of any potential wrongdoing within their company. This provision prohibits an employer from taking certain actions against informants who lawfully disclose private employer information to, among others, parties in a judicial proceeding involving a fraud claim. This Sarbanes-Oxley provision is not limited to securities-related offenses.

➢ **Defined Benefit Plan Notification Requirements** — Private companies that have a defined benefit plan must notify participants in writing at least thirty days in advance of any blackout periods under the plan. A blackout period is any period of more than three consecutive business days during which participants are restricted from diversifying assets in their account or obtaining plan loans or distributions.

➢ **White Collar Crime Liability and Penalties** — Sarbanes-Oxley adds criminal penalties and remedies, including criminal liability for altering or destroying documents to impede any federal investigation or bankruptcy case, and enhanced liability for white collar crimes and securities fraud. As with public companies, abuses now have more defined and severe penalties.

Sarbanes-Oxley Has Broad Ramifications for Private Companies Considering an IPO

Sarbanes-Oxley was targeted to large public companies, but will have a major impact on certain private companies. Specifically, private companies that are contemplating an IPO as an exit or growth strategy will have a lot of additional work as a result of Sarbanes-Oxley. That is because as soon as the company becomes public, it is required to comply with the more stringent Sarbanes-Oxley public company requirements. In fact, many of the Sarbanes-Oxley provisions apply when the company files a registration statement under the Securities Act of 1933. Below are considerations that private companies should work through before contemplating an IPO:

➤ **Added Preparation Time** — Underwriters will likely expect private companies to anticipate Sarbanes-Oxley requirements and to have put forth steps to comply prior to the time that a registration statement is filed with the SEC. This will add time to the IPO process. Net, any private company that is planning on going public should start early and develop plans to comply with Sarbanes-Oxley.

➤ **Higher Expenses** — Sarbanes-Oxley public company requirements are much more involved than they are for a privately held business. Becoming Sarbanes-Oxley compliant will add meaningful expense to an IPO. Large public companies claim they spend millions to comply with Sarbanes-Oxley. Small public companies can expect to spend hundreds of thousands of dollars (and possibly more) to comply with Sarbanes-Oxley. Private companies that plan on going public should establish a budget to comply with Sarbanes-Oxley.

➤ **More Distractions** — Sarbanes-Oxley necessitates more meeting time with lawyers, accountants, and the board for administration and compliance. This can take precious time away from important business-building activities.

➤ **Infrastructure Changes** — A company may need infrastructure changes. For example, with Sarbanes-Oxley, a public company must have a completely independent audit committee with appropriate financial expertise.

➤ **Independent Board**—Some venture capital backed companies have hand-picked boards. They may need to change their boards so that they have a majority of members who are truly independent.

➤ **Financial Reporting Documentation** — Sarbanes-Oxley's Section 404 requires management to document and evaluate internal controls and procedures for financial reporting. This detail work was absent in the past in most private companies and some public companies.

➢ **Elimination of Senior Officer Loans** — Sarbanes-Oxley eliminates loans to management. The past practice of loaning money to key executives to purchase shares before an IPO will no longer be available. This same Sarbanes-Oxley loan exclusion provision affects (eliminates) a previous practice of loaning money as a recruiting tactic so that key executives could purchase a home in costly cities such as San Francisco and New York that have high housing costs.

Customers May Require Sarbanes-Oxley

Certain private companies may experience pressure to comply with or partially comply with Sarbanes-Oxley, even though they are not legally required to do so. Private companies that have large, publicly traded customers are more likely to experience pressure to comply with some or all of the Sarbanes-Oxley requirements. These private companies may see Sarbanes-Oxley requirements show up in key supplier programs for vendors.

If your company has banks or other financially oriented customers, they may expect your company to be wholly or partially Sarbanes-Oxley compliant, even if you are a private company. These financially oriented customers may perceive Sarbanes-Oxley as a means to reduce their exposure and risk with suppliers.

Private companies that raise capital are more likely to see increases in due diligence in areas that are specific to Sarbanes-Oxley. Sarbanes-Oxley requirements that investors may be looking for include board independence, no insider loans, auditor independence, a code of conduct and ethics, among others.

Private companies that work for the government may also be required to become partially or wholly Sarbanes-Oxley compliant.

Sarbanes-Oxley Best Practices: Provisions to Consider

Several Sarbanes-Oxley provisions can serve as best practices that well-run private companies may want to incorporate into their business practices. These enhanced private company corporate governance practices, particularly accounting controls, will not eliminate the possibility of fraud or embezzlement. However, they could reduce the likelihood or severity of such acts. Specific Sarbanes-Oxley areas for private companies and their boards to consider include but are not limited to the following:

➢ **Establish an Independent Board** — A truly independent board will have a majority of outside (independent) directors (this excludes family members, VCs, company accountants, lawyers, and the like). Independent directors are often more objective. Plus, they can improve board candidate recruiting efforts and the quality of board members. Highly qualified board candidates could prefer an independent board, especially candidates who serve or have served on a public company board.

➢ **Implement a Code of Conduct and Ethics**—A code of conduct and ethics should be a written document. It should be communicated to the organization and board members on a periodic basis. An example of a code of conduct and ethics is provided in Chapter 10 and in Appendix 3. A code of conduct and ethics helps instill the right guidelines for board members and senior management. It can also positively affect the culture of an organization. It is a good idea to have policies that mandate compliance with applicable laws and that deter wrongdoing. It may be worth adding in the code of ethics, policies on conflicts of interest, confidentiality, compliance, and fair dealing, among others. These will be covered in more depth later on in this chapter. More important than drafting the policies is to ensure that employees are aware of them and that they are properly enforced. In addition to establishing good business practices, if a private company has appropriate policies in place and evidence that those policies are known and adhered to, it is in a much better legal position if a lawsuit were to evolve that involves unethical behavior claims.

➢ **Develop Financial Reporting Standards** — The duties of care and loyalty are the same in a private company as they are in a public company. It is good business practice for a private company to establish Sarbanes-Oxley-like standards for auditor independence, financial statement preparation, and auditing. In addition to reducing the potential for fraud, this could reduce potential litigation exposure. For example, if a private company is being sued for financial mismanagement, having an independent audit committee with a financial board expert would likely help the company to defend its case.

➢ **Eliminate Loans to Directors and Officers** — It is a good idea to reduce the potential for conflicts that could arise from extending loans to executive officers of the company.

➢ **Restrict Auditors to Financial Reporting Work Exclusively** — Prohibiting auditors from doing non-audit work could reduce the potential for a conflict of interest.

➢ **Review D&O Insurance Policies**—As a result of Sarbanes-Oxley, D&O insurance has changed dramatically. Thus, companies should periodically review their D&O insurance policy. This is covered in Chapter 12, *Protect Your Board Members.*

In 2002, several large, prominent corporations such as Enron, Rite Aid, WorldCom, and Tyco faced fraud and other serious legal charges that questioned the role of an independent board, particularly as it relates to the audit function and accurately reporting financials. As a result, Sarbanes-Oxley has established comprehensive changes to an audit committee's makeup, requirements, and charter. An overview of these changes follows.

The Audit Committee

An increasing climate of disclosure is impacting broadly traded, public company boards. Post-Sarbanes-Oxley, all broadly traded public companies require an independent audit committee (with required expertise, a charter, and autonomy). In large publicly traded companies, the audit committee will need to undergo significant changes, especially in finding members who are qualified (financial experts) and independent. The SEC defines an audit committee financial expert as an individual who has:

➤ An understanding of GAAP and financial statements;
➤ The ability to assess the application of GAAP principles in connection with accounting estimates, accruals, and reserves;
➤ Experience preparing, auditing, analyzing, or evaluating financial statements comparable to the breadth and complexity of the company's financials;
➤ An understanding of internal controls and procedures for financial reporting; and
➤ An understanding of audit committee functions.

There are tools available online that can help find financial experts. One such tool is available through the American Institute of Certified Public Accountants (AICPA) Audit Committee Effectiveness Center (www.aicpa.org/audcommctr). There are useful tools including an Audit Committee toolkit which includes checklists, questions, reports, and guidelines to help audit committees achieve best practices.

Ultimately, the audit committee is responsible for the completeness and accuracy of the company's disclosures. The audit committee is responsible for monitoring the internal financial reporting and audit processes. It focuses on accounting and internal control issues. It seeks to prevent audit issues from occurring. The audit committee should also address emerging issues that have a direct or indirect impact on a company's control environment, financial reporting, and the audit process.

The Enron disaster reinforced the importance of the audit committee to operate with autonomy and without conflicts. The audit committee should ensure a "no surprises" environment. It should identify if management is reporting operations in a reasonable way, one that enables a satisfactory response to any SEC inquiry into earnings management. Needless to say, the independent auditors must truly be "independent."

The audit committee should have an audit review meeting with the auditors without management present. This will enable the audit committee to ask directly if there are any disagreements with management on any topics or areas of the business. The audit review meetings should have no pre-planned length. Preferably, they should be held before scheduled board meetings so that time pressures do not preclude any issues from full exploration. The audit committee should have an easy to comprehend charter. Specific sections to consider including in an audit committee charter are as follows:

❖ **Role of the Audit Committee** — The audit committee should be independent (appointed by the board, not the CEO) to perform the functions required by law or regulation to perform and to assist the board in fulfilling its responsibility to oversee the company's accounting and financial reporting processes and the audits of the company's financial statements; the adequacy of the company's internal control over financial reporting; the integrity of its statements; the qualifications and independence of the company's independent auditor; the appointment, retention, and performance of the company's independent auditor, and the company's compliance with legal and regulatory requirements.

❖ **Qualifications and Appointment of Members**—This section should specify that each member be financially literate, with at least one member having had accounting and related financial management expertise. This section should also include the number of members on the committee and a requirement that members do not serve simultaneously on too many other company boards and their committees.

❖ **Authority and Responsibility** — This section should specify the specific authorities and responsibilities of the audit committee and be related to the role section discussed above. This is a very comprehensive area. As such, you should have experts on Sarbanes-Oxley help you with specifics.

❖ **Relationship with Independent and Internal Auditors** — This section should specify the relationships among independent auditors, internal auditors, the audit committee, management, and the board. Clear policies for hiring the independent auditor should be specified. They should include a truly independent relationship and the absence of any conflicts of interest.

❖ **Limitation on Audit Committee's Role** — This section should specify any audit committee limitations. An example would be that the audit committee is in an oversight capacity. As such, it does not provide expert or special assurances as to the company's financial statements; nor does it provide professional certification as to the independent auditor's work.

❖ **Evaluation** — This section should specify that the Audit committee will conduct an annual evaluation of its performance. It should also define the process for the annual evaluation.

Enron: Where Was the Board?

With respect to corporate governance for a broadly traded, public company, the Enron situation raised the question: "Where was the board?" John Smale, former Chairman of the Board of General Motors and CEO of Procter & Gamble, expressed a well-thought-out point of view on this subject (quoted below from a letter he wrote to the Honorable Rob Portman, Congressman from the Second District in Ohio). This letter was provided to the author and is used with permission:

Many issues are in the process of being examined as a result of the collapse of Enron. Congressional committees and others are looking at a variety of things—oversight of accountants, safeguarding 401K's, the influence of stock options on executive decisions, possible conflict of interest on the role analysts play, and others.

One issue that certainly will draw inquiry is the role the Enron Board played, or perhaps more accurately didn't play, in what happened.

There seems to be a general sense that a board of directors ought to know, in its own right, about a company's operations in enough detail to prevent, before the fact, mistakes of the magnitude that occurred at Enron. I believe, by and large, this may be an unrealistic assumption. Independent—or outside—Directors' knowledge of company activities is dependent principally on what Management discloses to the board. That information, together with the advice of the outside auditor, forms the basis of the board's fundamental understanding of the affairs of the company.

Generally, this system works well because management discusses all of the relevant information about the business with the board. But, sometimes it fails. And, after the fact, the board is faced with the question, "Where was the board?" The General Motors board asked itself this question a decade ago. As a result, the GM board created a series of some 28 procedures or guidelines designed to formally set out the specific actions for which the board and the board's committees were responsible in their duty to oversee the conduct of the business. Today, most boards of large companies have similar procedures.

But, there are a couple of other steps that, in my opinion, would further strengthen the oversight ability of a board of directors.

The first and most important would be to select the board's Chairman from among the independent directors on the board. This procedure is common in some countries such as the United Kingdom, but is relatively rare in the United States. And, it's an idea that is not warmly received by most

CEOs who are also Chairman of their company's board because it implies a sharing of some of the CEO's powers. But, if the purpose of a board is to represent the shareholders in overseeing Management's conduct of the business, such a structure seems considerably more logical than having the board chaired by a manager who is also the subject of such oversight.

Furthermore, it can create, in my opinion, a different tone to the board's activities...a more rigorous oversight climate in the board's approach to its responsibilities. The Chairman of the Board, working together with the CEO, would set the board's agendas, as well as conduct the board meetings. With an independent director as chairman, the board becomes responsible for its own constituency; selecting, with input from the CEO, its own members. It becomes responsible for its own governance guidelines, the charter of each board committee, etc.

In essence, a different attitude is created—one in which outside Directors see themselves not only as advisors and consultants to Management, but with the understanding they are individually, and as a whole, responsible for how well Management runs the business.

A further change that I believe is worth considering would see the outside auditors report to the board. In theory, that is the case today. In fact, in most companies, the shareholders vote to confirm the appointment of an outside auditor. But in practice, the real client of the auditing firm is the Management of the company. I believe the client should, in fact, be the Audit Committee of the board. Certainly, the financial staff of the company must work closely with the outside auditor. But, the basic relationship and the reporting responsibility should be directly to the board through the Audit Committee.

Would these changes avoid a future disaster like Enron? Perhaps not. But, I believe they would help. Certainly they would improve the opportunity for the board of directors to better execute its oversight responsibility to the shareholders.

John Smale eloquently makes the point for independent committees and Sarbanes-Oxley requires that the audit committee be independent.

The Importance of Integrity

Unfortunately, even though Sarbanes-Oxley has merit, it will not stop unethical management or board members from wrongdoing. One of the best steps you can take to prevent fraud and other board member abuses is to follow a key practice of Step 1 *(Right Team)*. *Namely, hire board members with high integrity who will inherently live up to a code of conduct and high ethical standards.*

CONCLUSIONS

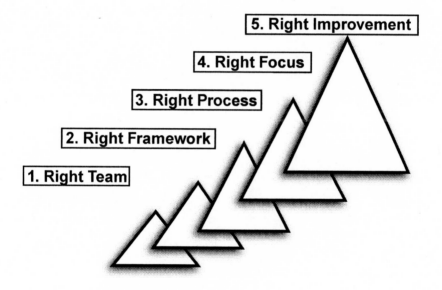

5. Right Improvement

4. Right Focus

3. Right Process

2. Right Framework

1. Right Team

24. Conclusions

"I wasted time, and now doth time waste me."

—William Shakespeare, Elizabethan playwright whose dramatic works provided profound insights into human nature

24. Conclusions

Creating or improving a board is not simple. Obviously, there is a lot of hard work involved. However, the effort should pay big dividends. In a nutshell, the 5 Steps will make it easier for you. It all starts with taking the initiative to take the first step. Hopefully, the ideas in this book will make your journey and business more successful:

Step 5: Right Improvement
Purposefully monitor then develop effective board improvement plans.

Step 4: Right Focus Focus board discussions on strategy and policy issues (doing the right things).

Step 3: Right Process Prepare for and organize meetings with discipline and rigor (doing things right). Build trust through open communication.

Step 2: Right Framework Set up the right independent board for your business needs. Establish clear expectations, fair compensation and insurance.

Step 1: Right Team Recruit a team of experts who are most qualified to help your business achieve its long-term vision, objectives, and goals.

APPENDIX AND RESOURCES

"To the illuminated mind the whole world sparkles."

— Ralph Waldo Emerson, American author, a potent force in thought during the nineteenth century and beyond

Appendix 1. Sample Board Search Description

Peak-Performance, Inc.
Board Search Description
(Created July 2004)

Our Need

- Peak-Performance's board has been an invaluable source of independent expertise and advice. Our objectives and mission are challenging and evolving and we are seeking a fourth outside board expert to help our company reach its next level of success. Specifically, the company is contemplating an IPO and afterwards plans to evaluate several complementary business acquisition opportunities.
- We recognize the value of a financial executive who has already faced similar challenges to what we expect to confront. Thus, we desire a board candidate who has hands-on experience with acquisitions and/or IPOs. Related expertise in hiring and overseeing investment bankers would be very beneficial.
- Familiarity with and working knowledge of Sarbanes-Oxley is a must.
- Prior board experience preferred but not essential.

Our Business

- A private, closely held company since inception (established in 1987) with headquarters in Cincinnati and sales offices in New York and Philadelphia.
- Leading niche player in physician office-based targeted media (see Statement of Purpose document that follows). Created and installed over 80,000 informational displays that reach over 50 million U.S.-based health-conscious consumers each year (see company brochures).

- Award-winning company (#23 in *Inc.* magazine's 500 Fastest Growing Private Companies List, Cincinnati Chamber of Commerce, Small Business of the Year).
- High organic growth (29 percent average per year) with approximately $31 million in sales and seventy-five employees.
- Results-oriented, entrepreneurial culture that lives by its principles (see attached Statement of Purpose).
- Excellent customer satisfaction and repeat business. Eleven of the top twenty pharmaceutical companies are clients (all are *Fortune 500* companies). Seven have been customers for over eight years.
- Strong balance sheet and fourteen-year track record of profitability. Equity is internally owned.
- Balanced and experienced management team in all key functional areas but no acquisitions or IPO experience.
- Have a leading position in a growing market segment and are seeking to aggressively grow through acquisitions, post-IPO with the goal being to dominate the office-based physician targeted media market.

An Overview of Our Current Board

- Established in 1991.
- Currently four members (CEO plus three independent members). The independent members have found our board to be a rewarding, engaging learning experience and helpful to their own careers. Current board members include:
  - The CEO of the company (CEO since the company was founded, fourteen years ago)
  - Former president of a large and successful competitive firm that was sold (ten years high-growth business expertise in the same industry)
  - Retired senior pharmaceutical marketing executive (thirty years' related customer experience and currently Chair of a start-up company)
  - Seasoned operations executive (eighteen years' operations expertise in an unrelated but highly reputable business)

Board Expectations Overview

- The Board Constitution provides clear expectations for board members. An overview of those expectations is reflected herein.
- The CEO will keep all board members informed between meetings and will send an organized board report before meetings with ample time to prepare.
- Typically, the board will meet four times a year for half-day morning meetings.
- It is expected that board members will be available for occasional phone conferences and infrequent emergency meetings, as appropriate.
- Three-year renewable term with annual review process (covered in Board Constitution, a separate document).
- Board members:
  - Are responsible and committed to the business.
  - Attend all meetings (ample advance notice provided).
  - Punctual and prepared for every meeting.
  - Demonstrate a proficient and solid understanding of the business, markets, and competitive landscape.
  - Are accessible in between meetings, as needed (voice conference, etc., approximately five hours per quarter).
  - Offer expert, objective, and honest advice. We want you to be straightforward and apolitical.
  - Express point of view firmly but not harshly.
  - Challenge the CEO with the goal to help the business and to support the long-term interests of the shareholders.
  - Do not micromanage—board members address strategy and policy issues and do not lead or manage the day-to-day business.
  - Identify opportunities and risks and contribute to solving strategic problems.
  - Help the company invent. Bring fresh ideas and new points of view for the CEO and management team to consider.

- Do not become "stale" (energy and enthusiasm remain high).
- Show initiative by constantly looking for ways to improve the business.
- Work well with other board members by respecting their opinions, not dominating the meetings, and listening to and building upon suggestions.
- Help the CEO network (i.e. identify good investment bankers, etc.).
- Hold the CEO accountable and are focused on improving the company's results, in part by ensuring management is accountable to those results.
- Are familiar with and in complete agreement with all of the terms and provisions of the Company's Code of Conduct and Ethics (included as an attachment).
- Help with succession/exit plans, as appropriate.
- Hold all discussions and information in complete confidence (also covered in the Code of Conduct and Ethics; see Appendix 3).

Board Compensation

- $2,000 per meeting attended (typically four per year).
- $7,500 yearly retainer.
- Meaningful phantom stock plan to share in long-term upside potential based upon performance over time with stock conversion options (if and when an IPO or exit occurs).
- All reasonable travel and meeting expenses.

Note: Peak-Performance, Inc. is a fictitious company that is used as an example throughout this book. The name *Peak-Performance Inc.,* was made up by the author and is not intended to be linked or associated with a real company. Any similarities are purely coincidental.

PEAK-PERFORMANCE, INC.

PURPOSE

To be recognized as *the* company where ideas are born, promises are kept and people look forward to work every day

MISSION

To become the leading health care media company by the end of the decade

WISDOM CORE VALUES

Wins - We thoroughly understand and fulfill customer, teammate, and supplier needs to ensure everyone wins

Integrity - We hire people with integrity who are intuitively service-minded, have a passion for excellence and who exude a positive attitude

Supportive Environment - We foster a fun, learning, and team-based environment

Dedication to Quality - We continually improve and strive for perfection so that our results become legendary

Ongoing Relationships - We develop long-lasting relationships of mutual trust

Magnified Value - We add measurable value to everything we do

Created November 1988. CBA 5/01—07

Appendix 2. Sample Board Constitution

Peak-Performance, Inc.
Board Constitution
(Created May 1993, last amended August 2004)

Statement of Purpose

- ❖ To maximize long-term profitability and shareholder value.
- ❖ To help Peak-Performance, Inc. achieve its mission, and long-term goals.
- ❖ To provide an invaluable source of outside, informed, and independent stimulation and advice that helps the company reach its next level of success.
- ❖ To ensure a disciplined strategic planning approach is deployed that encompasses client needs, the company's competitive situation, market position, external trends, and financial performance.
- ❖ To help the CEO make key decisions that affect the overall strategic direction of the company.
- ❖ To hold the CEO accountable to the plan and related results.
- ❖ To ensure appropriate company policies are in place and enforced.
- ❖ To serve as a court of appeals to senior management.
- ❖ To ensure a prudent and effective succession plan is in place.
- ❖ To assist the company in opening doors for opportunities (help network).

Board Parameters

- ❖ **Independent Members**—The board will have independent experts who have no inside or direct affiliation or conflicts with the company (excludes employees, family members, suppliers, and the like). A majority of members will be independent.
- ❖ **Number of Members** — The board will contain no less than three and no more than six members. There will be no more than

two inside members (CEO and one other, if needed). A majority of independent members will be maintained at all times.

- ❖ ***New Members** — New board members will require the majority approval of the shareholders (assumes Peak-Performance, Inc. remains a closely held business).

- ❖ **Chair** — The CEO will act as the board Chair. The Chair will preside over meetings and be responsible for establishing the agenda with input from the board.

- ❖ **Secretary** — The Chair will designate a Secretary whose responsibility will be to record all of the board minutes.

- ❖ **Meetings** — The board will meet four to five times a year for half-day morning meetings.

- ❖ **Attendance** — It is expected that all board members will attend all meetings (unless there is a true emergency). Board members are to be punctual and come prepared for every meeting. Board members are also expected to be available for occasional phone conferences and infrequent emergency meetings, as appropriate.

- ❖ **Communication** — The Chair is responsible for sending an organized board report before meetings and for keeping all board members informed between meetings.

- ❖ ***Voting Protocol** — The board will use an established voting process. Specifically, board topics, actions, or resolutions requiring a vote will start with an open discussion. After the open discussion, the Chair will call for a motion. If a motion is made, the Chair will then ask for a second to the motion. Objections will be considered and discussed. A verbal count of all those in favor and all those opposing the motion will be summarized. The vote will be concluded with a declaration that the motion has been accepted or rejected, contingent upon the vote.

- ❖ ***Majority Rules** — A majority of member's votes will rule.

- ❖ ***Split Votes** — If there is a tie, the Chair will cast the deciding vote.

- ❖ ***Recorded** — Anything that is voted on will be recorded by the Secretary and reflected in the minutes.

- ❖ **Code of Conduct and Ethics** — Each board member will be familiar with and in agreement with all of the terms and provisions of the Company's Code of Conduct and Ethics ("Code," see attached). Annually, each board member will be asked to certify that he or she is in compliance with the Code.

- ❖ **Board Terms** — Board terms will be for three years. Contingent upon satisfactory performance, they are renewable indefinitely up until retirement age is reached.
- ❖ **Retirement** — There is mandatory retirement at age seventy-five.
- ❖ **Board Evaluations** — Every board member will undergo an annual performance review process (see the Board Evaluation Form in Appendix 6). If performance is below an average of a "5" rating, the board member will be asked to resign.
- ❖ *Committees — There will be no committees.

*Not recommended for an advisory board

Board Member Role Description — Every Member:

- ❖ Is responsible and committed to the business.
- ❖ Attends all meetings and is punctual and prepared for every meeting.
- ❖ Demonstrates a proficient and solid understanding of the business, markets, and competitive landscape.
- ❖ Is accessible in between meetings, as needed (voice conference, etc., approximately five hours per quarter).
- ❖ Offers expert, objective and honest advice.
- ❖ Is straightforward and apolitical. Expresses own point of view firmly but not harshly. Challenges the CEO with the goal to help the business and to support the long-term interests of the shareholders.
- ❖ Does not micromanage — addresses strategy and policy issues and does not lead or manage the day-to-day business.
- ❖ Brings fresh ideas and new points of view for the CEO and management team to consider.
- ❖ Does not become "stale" (energy and enthusiasm remain high).
- ❖ Shows initiative by constantly looking for ways to improve the business.

- ❖ Works well with other board members and management, in part by respecting their opinions and not dominating board meetings. Further, demonstrates a willingness to work with other members by listening to and building upon suggestions.
- ❖ Identifies opportunities and risks and contributes to solving strategic problems.
- ❖ Helps the CEO network.
- ❖ Holds the CEO accountable and is focused on improving the company's results, in part by ensuring management is accountable to those results.
- ❖ Participates in and is receptive to an annual evaluation (see Board Evaluation Form in Appendix 6).
- ❖ Conducts an annual review of the CEO's performance (see CEO Evaluation Form in Appendix 8).
- ❖ Is familiar with and in complete agreement with all of the terms and provisions of the Company's Code of Conduct and Ethics (included as an attachment).
- ❖ Helps with succession/exit plans, as appropriate.
- ❖ Holds all discussions and information in complete confidence (also covered in the Code of Conduct and Ethics; see Appendix 3).

Appendix 3. Sample Code of Conduct and Ethics

Peak-Performance, Inc.
Code of Conduct and Ethics
(Adopted August, 2002)

The Board of Directors of Peak-Performance, Inc., an Ohio corporation, has adopted this Code of Conduct and Ethics ("Code") to promote: honest and ethical conduct, including fair dealing and the ethical handling of conflicts of interest; compliance with applicable laws and governmental rules and regulations; full, fair, accurate, timely, and understandable disclosure; and to ensure the protection of the Company's legitimate business interests, including Company opportunities, assets, and confidential information.

All employees, officers, and directors of the Company are expected to be familiar with the Code and to adhere to those principles and the procedures set forth in the Code that apply to them. For purposes of this Code, the "Code of Ethics Contact Person" will be:

- For each member of the Board of Directors: the Chair, Chief Executive Officer, or Chief Financial Officer.
- For Director-level or higher employees (e.g., Vice President of Operations, Director of Product Development, etc.): the Chief Executive Officer.
- For all other employees: the Director of the department in which they are employed.

Integrity—Consistent with Peak-Performance Inc.'s WISDOM principles, each employee, officer, and director owes a duty to the Company to act with integrity. Integrity requires, among other things, being honest, candid, truthful, and free from deception in all actions. This applies to observing laws and governmental rules and regulations, accounting standards, Company policies, and adhering to a high standard of business ethics.

Conflicts of Interest — A "conflict of interest" occurs when an individual's private interest interferes or appears to interfere in any way with the interests of the Company as a whole. A conflict of interest can arise when an employee, officer, or director takes actions or has interests that may make it difficult to perform his or her Company work objectively and effectively.

For example, a conflict of interest would arise if an employee, officer, or director (or a member of his or her family), receives improper personal benefits as a result of his or her position in the Company. Any material transaction or relationship that could reasonably be expected to give rise to a conflict of interest should be discussed with the Code of Ethics Contact Person.

This Code does not attempt to describe all possible conflicts of interest that could develop. Potential or real conflict of interest situations should always be discussed with the Code of Ethics Contact Person. Anything that would present a conflict for an employee, officer, or director would likely also present a conflict if it involved a family member. Clear conflict of interest situations involving employees, officers, and directors in supervisory positions or who have discretionary authority may include, but are not limited to the following:

- Any significant ownership interest in any supplier, competitor, or customer;
- Any outside business activity that detracts from an individual's ability to devote appropriate time and attention to their responsibilities with the Company;
- Any consulting or employment relationship with any supplier or competitor;
- Being in the position of supervising, reviewing, or having any influence on the job evaluation, pay, or benefit of any immediate family member;
- The receipt of non-nominal gifts or excessive entertainment from any person or company with which the Company has current or prospective business dealings; and

- Selling anything to the Company or buying anything from the Company, except on the same terms and conditions as comparable employees, officers, or directors are permitted to purchase or sell.

Compliance & Accuracy — It is the Company's policy to comply with all applicable laws, rules, and regulations. It is the personal responsibility of each employee, officer, and director to adhere to the standards and restrictions imposed by those laws, rules, and regulations.

It is the Company's policy that all transactions will be accurately reflected in its books and records. This means that falsification of books and records and the creation or maintenance of any off-the-record bank accounts are strictly prohibited. Employees are expected to record all transactions accurately in the Company's books and records and to be honest and forthcoming with the Company's internal and independent auditors.

Company Opportunities—Employees, officers, and directors owe a duty to the Company to advance the Company's business interests when the opportunity to do so arises. Employees, officers, and directors are prohibited from taking (or directing to a third party) a business opportunity that is discovered through the use of corporate property, information, or position, unless the Company has already been offered the opportunity and turned it down. More generally employees, officers, and directors are prohibited from using corporate property, information, or position for personal gain and from competing with the Company. Sometimes the line between personal and Company benefits is difficult to draw, and sometimes there are both personal and Company benefits in certain activities. Employees, officers, and directors who intend to make use of Company property or services in a manner not solely for the benefit of the Company should consult beforehand with the Code of Ethics Contact Person.

Confidentiality — In carrying out the Company's business, employees, officers, and directors often learn confidential or proprietary information about the Company, its customers, clients, suppliers, or joint venture parties. Employees, officers, and directors must maintain the confidentiality of all information so entrusted to them, except when disclosure is authorized or legally mandated. Confidential or proprietary information of the Company, and of other companies, includes any non-public information that would be harmful to the relevant company or useful or helpful to competitors if disclosed.

Fair Dealing — The Company cares how results are obtained; not just that they are obtained. We have a history of succeeding through consistently applying the same high ethical standards to every person and situation. We do not seek competitive advantage through unfair business practices. Each employee, officer, and director should endeavor to deal fairly with the Company's customers, clients, service providers, suppliers, and employees. No employee, officer, or director should take unfair advantage of anyone through manipulation, misrepresentation of material facts, or any unfair dealing practice.

Reporting Violations—The Company encourages employees, officers, and directors to report violations and make appropriate suggestions regarding the business practices of the Company. Specifically, any employee, officer, or director who becomes aware of any existing or potential violation of this Code is required to notify the Code of Ethics Contact Person promptly. Failure to do so is a violation of this Code.

Employees, officers, and directors are expected to report promptly to The Code of Ethics Contact Person, suspected violations of law, and the Company's policies (including this Code) so that the Company can take corrective action. No action may be taken or threatened against an employee, officer, or director for reporting violations, or making suggestions in conformity with the procedures described above, unless, the employee, officer, or director acts with willful disregard of the truth.

Appendix 4. Sample Board Orientation & Training Agenda

Peak-Performance, Inc.
Board Orientation & Training Agenda

May 7, 2005

8:30   **Introduction to Company (CEO)**
- **Review Board Statement of Purpose**
- **Review Board Constitution**
- **Review Code of Conduct and Ethics (Confidentiality)**
- **Introduce Key Managers (see bios sent with orientation package)**

9:15   **Tour (CEO)**
- **Overall Headquarters**
- **Marketing & Sales**
- **Operations**
- **Product Development**
- **Finance**
- **Customer Care Center**

10:00 **Break**

10:15 **Review of Strategic Plan (CEO)**
- **Purpose, Mission and Core Values**
- **SWOTS**
- **Unique Business Model**
- **Key Strategic Initiatives**
- **Objectives and Goals**
- **Measures, Benchmarks, and Action Plans (Balanced Scorecard)**
- **Questions?**

12:15 Lunch

- CFO (Claire Voyant) and EVP Product Development (John Gadget) will join us

1:00 Financial Orientation (Claire Voyant)

- Historical (balance sheet, income statement)
- Projections (balance sheet, income statement, cash flows)
- Questions?

2:15 Wrap Up (CEO)

- Questions and Suggestions?

Appendix 5. Sample Board Meeting Agenda

Peak-Performance, Inc.
Board Meeting Agenda

April 15, 2005
7:30 a.m. to 12:00 p.m.
First Floor Conference Room

Meeting Objectives

- Decide go/no go on pursuing southeast acquisition opportunity (board vote)
- Provide feedback and ideas on strategic initiatives
  - New Product Plan
  - Technology Plan
- Review key performance measures
- Vote on Bank LOC increase
- Preview future meetings
  - Generate agenda ideas
  - Schedule 2nd quarter '06 meeting

Specific Agenda Items and Timeframes

7:30 Open discussion on southeast acquisition opportunity (preparation materials included in board package)
- How well does the prospect fit our strategy?
- What other opportunities/risks do you see?
- How is the cultural fit?
- Other suggestions, issues, or concerns?
- Vote on pursuing acquisition or not (pending board discussion—written resolution included with board package)

9:30 Break

9:45 Introduction to New Products Strategy and John Gadget (EVP Product Development)
- New Products Presentation by John Gadget, EVP of Product Development (please review New Product Plan and John's bio in board report)
- Q & A of John Gadget from board
- Board reactions to presentation and suggestions/builds on Peak-Performance New Product Plan

10:45 Strategic Thought Starter Discussion: "What is the company's plan to take advantage of new technology?"
- Do we have a good handle on the available technologies that can help our company grow?
- If not, how are we going to obtain them?
- What kind of ROI are we realizing from investments in technology?
- Reactions/suggestions to improve Technology Plan (included in board package)
- Networking opportunities—Does the board know of good technology strategy consultants?

11:30 Review of Quarterly Board Report
- Key measurement trends, benchmarks, and financials
- Any questions or suggestions?
- Vote on bank line of credit increase (resolution in board package)
- Board recommendations for future meeting topics

11:55 Wrap Up
- Schedule future meeting date (please bring your calendars). How does the second week of April 15, 2006 look?
- Next Steps (who does what and when)

Appendix 6. Sample Board Member Evaluation Form

Peak-Performance, Inc.
Board Member Effectiveness Evaluation
(Created 9/95, Last Improved 5/04)

Board Member's Name:

Date of Evaluation:

Evaluation Period (from, to):

Evaluator's Name (and signature):

Please rate yourself on each of the evaluation criteria below. This evaluation is intended to provide you with feedback and a point of discussion so that the board can continue to improve. Your responses will be kept confidential.

Evaluation Criteria	Weak			Meets				Peak		
	1	2	3	4	5	6	7	8	9	10
1. Focuses On Strategy/Policy										
2. Helps Invent										
3. Provides Expert Advice										
4. Knowledge of Business										
5. Prep/Attendance/Punctuality										
6. Initiative (Proactive)										
7. Integrity/Confidentiality										
8. Participation (Balanced)										
9. Works Well With Others										
10. Effectively Communicates										
11. Expresses Own POV										
12. Challenges Status Quo										
13. Helps Identify Opportunities										
14. Helps Solve Problems										
15. Helps Identify Risks										
16. Helps Network										
17. Offers Creative Suggestions										
18. Holds Management Accountable										
19. Helps With Succession/Exit Plan										
20. Business Results (Profits, etc.)										
21. Overall Evaluation										

Please provide any additional comments or perspective as appropriate (optional)

_____

_____

_____

_____

_____

_____

_____

_____

_____

_____

_____

_____

_____

Appendix 7. OBE Evaluation Form

Right Team: Step 1

Evaluation Criteria (Step 1)	Weak	Meets	Peak
➢ Ethics			
➢ Trust			
➢ Confidentiality			
➢ Commitment			
➢ Consistently High Output			
➢ Preparation			
➢ Participation			
➢ Number of Members			
➢ Outside:Inside Ratio (Independence)			
➢ Board Leadership			
➢ Balanced Team			
➢ Builds Upon Strengths			
➢ Complements Weaknesses			
➢ Quality of Expertise			
➢ Variety of Expertise			
➢ Works Well Together (fit)			
➢ Judgment of Board			
➢ Business Acumen of Board			
➢ Listening Ability of Board			
➢ Expression of Own POV			
➢ Invention/Creativity			
➢ Sensitivity to Family Issues			
➢ Sensitivity to High Growth			
➢ Organized Recruiting Effort			
➢ Board Competency Matrix			
➢ Member Role Description			
➢ Reference Checking			
➢ Ongoing Scouting			
➢ **Overall: Step 1**			

Right Framework: Step 2

Evaluation Criteria (Step 2)	<u>Weak</u>	<u>Meets</u>	<u>Peak</u>
➤ Right Board Structure			
➤ Overall Board Constitution			
➤ Statement of Purpose			
➤ Role Expectations			
➤ Board Parameters			
➤ Code of Conduct and Ethics*			
➤ Independent Committees*			
➤ Sarbanes-Oxley Compliance*			
➤ Short-Term Compensation			
➤ Long-Term Compensation			
➤ Insurance			
➤ **Overall: Step 2**			

* If appropriate (some items not recommended for an advisory board)

Right Process: Step 3

Evaluation Criteria (Step 3)	Weak	Meets	Peak
➤ Board Orientation			
➤ Orientation Fact Book			
➤ Orientation Checkup			
➤ Number of Meetings			
➤ Too Many Emergency Meetings			
➤ Preparation of Meetings			
➤ Length of Meetings			
➤ Meeting Objectives			
➤ Meeting Agendas			
➤ Meeting Organization			
➤ Meeting Dynamics			
➤ Written Meeting Summaries			
➤ Clear Meeting Action Steps			
➤ Information Flow (both ways)			
➤ Communication (in meetings)			
➤ Communication (outside)			
➤ Clear Voting Process*			
➤ **Overall: Step 3**			

* If appropriate (some items not recommended for an advisory board)

Right Focus: Step 4

Evaluation Criteria (Step 4)	Weak	Meets	Peak
➤ Strategic Plan Focus			
➤ Avoidance of Tactics			
➤ Focus on Right Priorities			
➤ Questions (15 Key Strategic)			
➤ Active Listening			
➤ CEO Boundaries Challenged			
➤ Quality of Advice			
➤ Fact Based Advice			
➤ Networking Advice			
➤ Receptivity to Advice			
➤ Fiduciary Responsibilities*			
➤ Monitoring Performance*			
➤ Asset Protection*			
➤ Management Oversight*			
➤ Legal Requirements*			
➤ Accountability*			
➤ Succession Plan			
➤ **Overall: Step 4**			

* If appropriate (some items not recommended for an advisory board)

Right Improvement: Step 5

Evaluation Criteria (Step 5)	Weak	Meets	Peak
➢ Member Performance			
➢ Member Improvement Plans			
➢ CEO Performance*			
➢ CEO Improvement Plan*			
➢ OBE Performance			
➢ Follow-up on OBE Evaluation			
➢ Recognition			
➢ Right Business Measures			
➢ Customer Satisfaction			
➢ Long-Term Profit Results			
➢ Shareholder Interests			
➢ Improving Company Value			
➢ Other Key Results			
➢ **Overall: Step 5**			

* If appropriate (some items not recommended for an advisory board)

Appendix 8. Sample CEO Evaluation Form

Peak-Performance, Inc.
CEO Evaluation
(Created 10/97)

CEO's Name: _____

Date of Evaluation: _____

Evaluation Period (from, to): _____

Board Evaluator's Name (and signature): _____

Please rate the CEO on each of the evaluation criteria below. This evaluation is intended to provide the CEO with feedback and a point of discussion so that the CEO can continue to improve. Responses will be shared in a consensus report. Your individual responses will be kept confidential.

Evaluation Criteria	Weak			Meets				Peak		
	1	2	3	4	5	6	7	8	9	10
1. Revenue Results										
2. Profit Results										
3. Enterprise Value Results										
4. Strategic Plan (right plan)										
5. Focuses on Strategy/Policy										
6. Leadership										
7. Quality of Executive Team										
8. Teamwork										
9. Open Communication/Trust										
10. Listening										
11. Integrity										
12. Rigor and Discipline										
13. Lives by Values/Culture										
14. Willingness to Improve/Learn										
15. Overall Effectiveness										

Please provide any additional comments or perspective as appropriate (optional)

_____
_____
_____
_____
_____
_____
_____
_____
_____
_____
_____
_____
_____
_____

Board Effectiveness Resources: Organizations

- **American Society of Corporate Secretaries**

  521 Fifth Avenue, 32nd Floor
  New York, NY 10175
  212-681-2000
  Web site: *www.ascs.org*

- **The Conference Board**

  845 Third Avenue
  New York, NY 10022
  212-759-0900
  Web site: *www.conference-board.org*

- **The Family Firm Institute**

  221 North Beacon Street
  Boston, MA 02135-1943
  617-789-4220
  Web site: *www.ffi.org*

- **National Association of Corporate Directors**

  1707 L Street NW, Suite 560
  Washington, DC 20036
  202-775-0509, ext. 215
  Web site: *www.nacdonline.org*

Board Effectiveness Resources:
Periodicals

- *Across the Board*

  The Conference Board
  845 Third Avenue
  New York, NY 10022
  212-759-0900
  Web site: *www.conference-board.org*

- *Board Member*

  BoardSource (formally the National Center for Nonprofit Boards)
  1828 L Street NW, Suite 900
  Washington, DC, 20036-5114
  202-452-6262
  Web site: *www.boardsource.org*

- *The Corporate Board*

  4440 Hagadorn Road
  Okemos, MI 48864
  517-336-1700
  Web site: *www.corporateboard.com*

- *Corporate Secretary*

  American Society of Corporate Secretaries
  521 Fifth Avenue, 32nd Floor
  New York, NY 100175
  212-681-2000
  Web site: *www.ascs.org*

- *Directorship*

  8 Sound Shore Drive
  Greenwich, CT 06830
  213-861-7000
  Web site: *www.directorship.com*

- *Director's Monthly*

  National Association of Corporate Directors
  1707 L Street NW, Suite 560
  Washington, DC 20036
  210-775-0509
  Web site: *www.nacdonline.org*

- *Harvard Business Review*

  Harvard Business School Publishing
  Corporate Customer Service Center
  60 Harvard Way, Box 230-5C
  Boston, MA 02163 USA
  Web site: *www.hbsp.harvard.edu*

- **Leader to Leader Institute**

  The Peter F. Drucker Foundation for Non-Profit
  Management
  320 Park Avenue, 3rd Floor
  New York, NY 10022
  212-224-1174
  Web site: *www.pfdf.org*

Board Effectiveness Resources:
Suggested Reading

Change

- *Managing at the Speed of Change*
  Daryl R. Connor
  Random House, 1992

- *Thriving on Chaos*
  Tom Peters
  Alfred A. Knopf, 1987

- *Who Moved My Cheese?*
  Ken Blanchard & Spencer Johnson
  Putnam Publishing Group, 1998

Family Business

- *Creating Effective Boards For Private Enterprises*
  John L. Ward
  Jossey-Bass Publishers, 1991

- *How to Choose and Use Advisors: Getting the Best Professional Family Business Advice*
  John L. Ward and Craig E. Aronoff
  Business Owners Resource, 1994

- *Keep the Family Baggage Out of the Family Business: Avoiding the Seven Deadly Sins That Destroy Family Businesses*
  Quentin J. Fleming
  Simon & Schuster, 2000

- *Outside Directors in the Family Owned Business Why, When, Who and How*
  Leon A. Danco & Donald J. Jonovic
  The Center For Family Business, 1981

- *Strategic Planning for the Family Business: Parallel Planning to Unify the Family and Business*
  Randel S. Carlock & John L. Ward
  Palgrave, 2001

HR & Employee Performance

- *How to Win Friends and Influence People*
  Dale Carnegie
  Pocket Books, 1994

- *Now, Discover Your Strengths*
  Marcus Buckingham & Donald O. Clifton
  Free Press, 2001

- *The HR Scorecard: Linking People, Strategy and Performance*
  Brian E. Becker
  Harvard Business School Press, 2001

- *The One-Minute Manager*
  Spencer Johnson & Ken Blanchard
  Berkley Publishing Group, 1993

- *Zapp! The Lightening of Empowerment*
  William C Byham, Ph.D.
  Harmony Books, 1991

Leadership

- *Good to Great*
  Jim Collins
  HarperBusiness, 2001

- *Leadership Is an Art*
  Max DePree
  Dell Publishing, 1989

- *Servant Leadership*
  Robert K. Greenleaf
  Paulist Press, 1991

- *Success Is a Choice*
  Rick Pitino
  Broadway Books, 1997

- *The 7 Habits of Highly Effective People*
  Stephen R. Covey
  Simon & Schuster, 1989

- *The 21 Irrefutable Laws of Leadership, Follow Them and People Will Follow You*
  John C. Maxwell
  Thomas Nelson, 1998

Miscellaneous

- *Facilitator's Guide to Participatory Decision-Making*
  Sam Kaner, Catherine Toldi, and Sara Fisk
  New Society Publishers, 1996

- *Flow*
  Mihaly Csikszentmihalyi
  Harper Perennial, 1991

- *How to Hold Successful Meetings: 30 Action Tips for Managing Effective Meetings*
  Paul R. Timm
  Career Press, 1997

- *Getting to Yes: Negotiating Agreements Without Giving In*
  Roger Fisher
  Penguin USA, 1991

- *I Know It When I See It, A Modern Fable About Quality*
  John Guaspari
  Amacom, 1985

Sales & Marketing

- *Marketing Warfare*
  Al Reis & Jack Trout
  McGraw-Hill, 1986

- *Solution Selling: Creating Buyers in Difficult Selling Markets*
  Michael T. Bosworth
  McGraw-Hill, 1994

- *The New Strategic Selling: The Unique Sales System Proven Successful By the World's Best Companies*
  Stephen E. Heiman
  Warner Books, 1998

- *What They Don't Teach You at Harvard Business School*
  Mark H. McCormack
  Bantam Books, 1984

Small Business

- *Growing a Business*
  Paul Hawken
  Simon & Schuster, 1987

- *Innovation and Entrepreneurship*
  Peter Drucker
  HarperBusiness, 1993

- *Jump Start Your Brain: Win More, Lose Less and Make More Money*
  Doug Hall
  F&W Publications, 2001

- *The E-Myth Revisited: Why Most Small Businesses Don't Work and What to Do about It*
  Michael E. Gerber
  HarperBusiness, 1995

Strategy

- *Beyond Entrepreneurship: Turning Your Business into an Enduring Great Company*
  James C. Collins & William C. Lazier
  Prentice-Hall

- *Built to Last: Successful Habits of Visionary Companies*
  James C. Collins & Jerry Porras
  HarperBusiness, 1997

- *Competitive Strategy*
  Michael E. Porter
  The Free Press, 1980

- *Corporate Lifecycles*
  Ichak Adizes
  Prentice-Hall, 1988

- *Perspectives on Strategy From The Boston Consulting Group*
  Edited by Carl W. Stern & George Stark Jr.
  John Wiley & Sons, 1998

- *Positioning: The Battle for Your Mind*
  Al Reis & Jack Trout
  McGraw-Hill, 1986

- *The Art of War*
  Sun Tzu
  Oxford University Press, 1984

- *The Goal: A Process for Ongoing Improvement*
  Eliyahu M. Goldratt & Jeff Cox
  Norton River Press Publishing, 1992

- *The Strategy-Focused Organization: How Balanced Scorecard Companies Thrive in the New Business Environment*
  Robert S. Kaplan & David P. Norton
  Harvard Business School Press, 2000

Index

313

T

About the Author

Mark Daly is currently founder/CEO of Daly Strategic Associates. He was founder/CEO of three high growth companies including:

- The Exam Room Network, the first and largest healthcare TV network in physician exam rooms;
- On Target Media, an Inc. Magazine 500 Fastest Growing Privately Held Company winner (# 23 in 1993) and winner of the Cincinnati Chamber of Commerce Small Business of the Year Award (1997);
- ProtoCall, LLC, a leading syndicated contract sales organization with over 400 employees.

Prior to leading these successful companies, Mr. Daly was a brand manager at Procter & Gamble.

Mr. Daly is a former member of the Board of Examiners for the Malcolm Baldridge National Quality Award. He has served on many boards and is a member of the Young Presidents Organization.

Mr. Daly is the producer and composer of Connections, a critically acclaimed CD of original music which includes performances by Grammy Award winning musicians. He received his undergraduate degree from Cornell University in Economics and his MBA in Strategic Planning and Marketing from the University of Pennsylvania's Wharton School of Business.

Printed in the United States
R1791000001B/R17910PG38561LVSX00003B/3}